THE REALLY,
REALLY CLASSY
DONALD TRUMP
QUIZ BOOK

THE REALLY, REALLY CLASSY DONALD TRUMP QUIZ BOOK

Complete, Unauthorized, Fantastic . . . and the Best!!

by

Jess M. Brallier
and
Richard P. McDonough

Little, Brown and Company

Boston $ Toronto $ London

FIRST EDITION

Other books by Brallier and McDonough
The Pessimist's Journal of Very, Very Bad Days
The Pessimist's Journal of Very, Very Bad Days of the 1980s

ISBN 0-316-10608-9

10 9 8 7 6 5 4 3 2 1

Published simultaneously in Canada by Little, Brown & Company (Canada) Limited

PRINTED IN THE UNITED STATES OF AMERICA

TO

Marvin Roffman, my kind of analyst
—RPM

Booksellers (just as it should be)
and attorneys (just in case)
—JMB

"It's a look,
it's an age,
it's a style,
it's a success."

—Donald Trump,
on Donald Trump

After a tour of the Trumps' Triplex Penthouse in Trump Tower, *New Statesman* magazine offers this definition of a Trump:

"*A man
whose front room
proved that
it really was possible
to spend
a million dollars
in Woolworth's.*"

THE REALLY,
REALLY CLASSY
DONALD TRUMP
QUIZ BOOK

FOREWORD

Each era has its greats, people who leave their mark on our lives. Great scientists like the Curies and Jonas Salk, whose work healed us; politicians and statesmen like Churchill, Roosevelt, and Gorbachev, who freed us from tyranny and fear; and builders like Nebuchadnezzar, who created a magnificent Babylon, Haussmann, who gave Paris its grand avenues, and Donald Trump, who gave us . . . more about that later.

Mr. Donald Trump, as we often call him, has been an inspiration to us. He has, in a curious way, saved our lives. In fact, you may want to ask yourself: Has he saved mine? Why? Because sometimes each of us feels down, inadequate, wanting. It is a tough world and sometimes it is hard to go on. Sometimes we are foolish and we feel particularly needy. That was the case for us.

What could we possibly do to redeem ourselves? we asked. Yeah, the first *Pessimist's Journal* had been fun, and the second even more fun, but my gosh, we're grown men, right?—we needed to get serious. We needed respect, the admiration of our betters, the esteem of hairdressers and bankers, the obsequiousness of waiters. In short, we needed class. So—okay, you see it coming, and you're right—what could have more class than to be associated with Mr. Class himself, Mr. Donald Trump?

You're right again—nothing could have more class, for he is the very definition of class, which is, by the way, along with "flair," one of the very favorite of all the words he knows. (We shouldn't be letting you know all this now because some of this very information is an answer to one of the questions inside, but if you're anything like us, and I'm sure you are, you will be too classy to take advantage and will have forgotten by the time you get to the question.) We thought if we could just get close to such a terrific guy, even in so inconsequential a way as this, we could learn something and lift ourselves up, help ourselves to get an adult view of life, get to see it as the serious and weighty matter that it is. And share what we learn with you.

Being realists, however, and knowing that everyone doesn't have the right genes or instincts for understanding and appreciating the complexities involved in The Life and Thought of The Donald (we call him that sometimes, too), we soon concluded that a palatable format would have to be contrived so that even the least of us (we mean you) could share our view of Mr. Donald Trump. And since TD himself has said that life is a game, we thought this question-and-answer format, with points awarded for the truly clever among us, would be the perfect way to get inside Mr. D (his help calls him that, sometimes, but we would hesitate to do so, ourselves). It has been a worthwhile if arduous task. We are grateful and fortunate that The Donald has so willingly shared so much of himself with all of us. From his Inspiring Book and the monthly and weekly magazines, to the daily newspapers, Donald has been very much with us for more than a decade.

CLASSY!

Some people might think his willingness to make major chunks of His Life and Thought available to ordinary people suggests that he is a needy person, that he is someone who has to see his name in print day after day after day to gather enough strength to roll out of bed. Some might scratch their heads over why a guy needs over one hundred rooms on three floors *to live in.* Others might think that The Donald is presumptuous to think that anyone would really care about the daily life a Swedish-Scot from the Bronx who builds startlingly vulgar buildings, is seen in the company of boxing promoters with alarmed hair, is distracted by very beautiful translators during a deal, and provides long-term venues for televised wrestling, not to mention his possessing the insouciance of a Friday-night singer in a New Jersey club. The truth could not be farther away. We are very, very interested, for this is an extraordinary man in an extraordinary time. (How extraordinary has this time been? Reagan, Bush, Drexel, Caspar, Watt, Ed Kosner; the return of capital punishment, plaids, and *Vanity Fair.* Need we say more? No? But we will.) Some have wondered if the declining wealth of The Donald and the possibility of...gods forbid...default, bankruptcy, and other plots against The Best might deflect our interest. If *you* wondered that, then you don't know Your Authors! We are nothing if not devoted. Now on to the work at hand.

As to the answers to the questions contained in the Quiz Book, we have had to rely on our own strong interest . . . okay, let's be honest . . . our almost idolatrous interest in The Donald to get what we might call Inside His Skin (only a metaphor). We think we have done a fantastic, even classy job of achieving just that; and so the answers to some of the questions are *what we think Mr. Donald Trump himself would give.* Others are part of the historic record. When taken together, we think they form a full and fantastic portrait of what it takes to be The Best.

In answering the questions, keep in mind one of the great truisms that have guided Mr. Donald Trump's life: Class tells. You don't have to get a high score. Life needs its losers, too. Remember what a Great American said: "...if it can't be fun, what's the point."

 [For you scholars, references to Trump: (1) *The Art of the Deal* is noted as T:TAOTD, and (2) Mr. Donald Trump is often referred to as The Donald or TD or DT or, in our most comfortable but perhaps too forward moments, as Donald.]

TrumpQuotes!!

♀ ♀ ♀ ♀ ♀ ♀ ♀ ♀ ♀ ♀ ♀ ♀ ♀ ♀ ♀ ♀

"I think it's upsetting to people that Donald and I have it all: We're young, we're healthy, we love our work and we have a good marriage and children on top of that! People can't stand that."
—Ivana

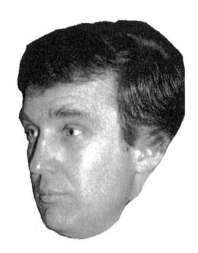

♂ ♂ ♂ ♂ ♂ ♂ ♂ ♂ ♂ ♂ ♂ ♂ ♂ ♂ ♂

"I can't believe I'm married. This is the prime time for me."
—The Donald, on girls (1990)

"My heart goes out to her. I have nuns praying for her."
—Chanel executive Catherine D'Alessio, on Ivana

FOR OUR READERS!!

This is a test. You will accumulate points as you proceed through the material. There is *not* a time limit! And there is *no* dress code! We, the editors, strongly suggest that a *very, very heavy dark ink pen* be used to enter your answers and points. (That way, you'll be unable to share this book. You'll then have to rush to the bookstore and buy more for your deserving friends and family members. They, in turn, will read this very same paragraph, and also use *a very, very heavy dark ink pen* and likewise be forced to buy more copies of this book for their co-workers, in-laws, and neighbors, and suddenly, BOOM!—in the Spirit of Trump, this is a great *deal* for us, the editors.)

Answers *almost* always run on the bottom of the same page as the question—in the publishing biz, they call that a "footer." (Watch out! Be careful! The answers are upside down.) When the answer's not contained in the upside-down footer (now that you're familiar with the terminology), you'll figure it out.

Scattered throughout the test are an assortment of TrumpQuotes, TrumpLightningBolts,

TrumpFacts, TrumpDialogue, TrumpMini-Features, TrumpTrivia, TrumpEtc. Some of these offer you, the reader, the opportunity to earn additional points—so you have to read *all* of them.

The questions reward you, the reader, with various amounts of points (some even penalize you with negative points, so be careful!). Most of the answers are grouped with a point system as in the following example:

> Answer #22: b) Mel Torme [correct, 10 points; wrong, 0 points]
> ____ points earned.   ____ running total.

So in the sample, if you indeed determined that the correct answer was "b) Mel Torme," enter "10" in the space next to "points earned." However, if you blew it—like, maybe you guessed Wayne Newton or somebody like that—enter "0" in the space next to "points earned." Wherever points are earned but not *exactly* as in the sample format, the points awarded will be obvious to any idiot. We, the editors, strongly suggest that you enter your points as you proceed through the test (thus, the "____ running total" entry provided in each answer), then total them at the end, because that's the TrumpWay of doing things.

Good luck! And remember: Be kind to your local bookseller and use the sure sign of a TrumpWinner—*a very, very heavy dark ink pen!!*

TRUMPFACT

1. TrumpFact! Fill in the TrumpBlank!

Trump claims that New York Times architecture critic Paul Goldberger is unqualified to judge his buildings because

_____

a. he never heard of Doug Flutie.
b. he lives in Olympia Tower.
c. he's friendly with Liz Smith.
d. he wears cheap suits.

2. In February 1990, during the week that the failed Trump marriage completely dominated the news, what other four events occurred?

a. Nelson Mandela was freed.
b. Orson Bean played Carnegie Hall.
c. East and West Germany surged toward reunification.
d. President George Bush traveled to Colombia to form an "anti-drug cartel."
e. Drexel Burnham filed for bankruptcy.
f. Jessica Lange ran off with Bert Convey.

Answer #2: a, c, d, and e [5 points for each correct choice; -3 penalty points for each one missed; 8 bonus points if you got all 4 right!] _____ points earned. _____ running total.

Answer #1: d. he wears cheap suits. [correct, 10 points, wrong, 0 points] _____ points earned. _____ running total.

3.

Serious students of The Donald will breeze through this one. The answers are all in T:TAOTD. Match the entry in column A with the right TrumpAssociation in column B!!

A

1. a huge and magnificent gold wreath
2. Roy Cohn
3. tallest building
4. Alan Greenberg
5. Barbara Walters
6. casino business
7. Ivana
8. Michael Milken
9. Leonard Lauder
10. Judith Krantz
11. Blanche "Blanchette" Sprague
12. Walter Hoving

B

a. a wonderful person
b. loyalty
c. less is more
d. a classic
e. a brilliant businessman
f. a brilliant guy
g. you've got to give it to her
h. ultimate symbol
i. she's got the biggest facility in town
j. never wastes time
k. huge, glamor, cash flow
l. totally honorable, totally classy

"They're all a bunch of con artists."

—The Donald's father, Fred, on England's Royal Family

"When the Queen of England is over in this country, they call my office to find out if they can use my helicopter...."

—The Donald

____ 12 correct] ____ points earned. ____ running total.

each correct answer, 0 points for each wrong answer; 20 bonus points if you got all

Answer #3: 1-c, 2-b, 3-h, 4-l, 5-a, 6-k, 7-j, 8-f, 9-e, 10-g, 11-d, 12-l [10 points for

TRUMPLIGHTNINGBOLT

"I discovered, for the first time but not the last, that politicians don't care too much what things cost. It's not their money."

"It's been a tough time for Drexel."

"If you want to buy something, it's obviously in your best interest to convince the seller that what he's got isn't worth very much."

4. True or False?!?

"They had what
Donald needed.
They're strict.
They're stern...that
school really built
him up in his forma-
tive years. He became
a captain, and he
marched in the Co-
lumbus Day parade.
He had medals on like
he won the war
singlehandedly."

—Fred "Father of The
Donald" Trump, on the
New York Military
Academy

                                                 TRUE   FALSE

A. Mayor Ed Koch said of The Donald, "Piggy, piggy, piggy."   ___   ___

B. Ivana Trump, claiming that she's so famous she's got exclusive rights to the name, in 1989 sues the manufacturer of "Ivana" lipstick for $10 million.   ___   ___

C. At an Altoona (Pa.) intersection, a billboard 1) asks "Do you think Ivana Trump should get more than $25 million?" and 2) provides 900 numbers so you can vote yes or no for *only* $1 per vote.   ___   ___

D. The Boyhood Home of The Donald at 85-14 Midland Parkway, Jamaica Estates, New York, is currently open to the public (reservations required!!).   ___   ___

E. The Birthplace of Ivana in Zlin, Czechoslovakia, is currently open to the public (including guided tours!!).   ___   ___

F. The Donald authorized, encouraged, and funded the publication of this book.   ___   ___

___ points earned. ___ running total.

Answer #4: A-True B-True C-True D-False E-True F-False [10 points for each correct answer; 0 points for each wrong answer, and -5 if you got "F" wrong!]

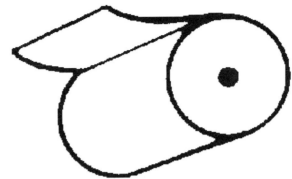

5.

Match the TrumpWow-er with the TrumpHome! Enter "TP" for the *Trump Princess* (yacht), "MAL" for Mar-a-Lago (estate, Palm Beach), or "TTP" for The Trump Tower Penthouse (a triplex!).

TrumpWow-er	enter "TP," "MAL," or "TTP"
A. size of a football field	——
B. weighs 1,767 tons	——
C. one bulletproof sauna	——
D. 11 double guest suites each with a complete audiovideo system (CD, stereo, VCR, color TV)	——
E. 80-foot-long living room	——
F. cinema with seating for 18	——
G. gold-*plated* bathroom fixtures and one *solid*-gold sink	——
H. two bomb shelters	——
I. 100 rooms	——
J. 210 telephones	——
K. a suede-lined vault	——
L. video games room	——
M. 12-foot waterfall	——
N. toilet paper embossed with the Trump symbol	——
O. 118 rooms	——
P. three waterfalls	——

[Running points earned. —— running total.

[5 points for each correct answer; 0 points for each wrong answer; 40 bonus points if you got every TrumpWow-er correct!]

Answer #5: A-TP B-TP C-TP D-TP E-TTP F-TP G-TP H-MAL I-TTP J-TP K-TP L-TP M-TTP N-TP O-MAL and TTP P-MAL

A TrumpManhattanMystery

Since, as The Donald claims, you'd never notice Grand Central Terminal if it wasn't for his reflecting-glass-skinned Grand Hyatt, just how the hell did all those people catch their trains home before the Hyatt was built? Or did they only start coming in from Connecticut after all that glass went up? And is that when the homeless first noticed Grand Central? Was there anyone there before? Or just people with pocket mirrors? No wonder the Penn Central went under. Wow! Really mysterious!

An Early Trump Warning!

It is 1968 and Donald Trump admits to having his eye on you, Manhattan!

DONALD
THE FORMATIVE YEARS

Some people have assumed that Donald Trump (we call him that here because he had not yet become The Donald or even Mr. Donald Trump at the time of which we speak) lived with a silver spoon in his mouth, that he spent all his time shopping for good deals while the rest of the young men were out working at soda fountains or helping out at home. While not quite a hod carrier, the young Donald was out learning the affordable housing business (so called because it afforded the owner of the housing a good living) from the front lines. He went out rent-collecting with father Fred. He learned that you never stand in front of a door when you knock at the apartment of someone who is in arrears of rent. The losers on the other side of the door, the oafs with bad instincts and bad genes, might resent your arrival just to get what's yours, and manifest their umbrage in some loser way. But his father told him that when you stood to the side of the door, only your hand was exposed to danger. Donald determined, however, that "this was not a world I found very attractive."

Some critics have suggested that it was the length of DT's fingers on his already short hands that gave rise to this attitude, but it is not so. Just as the movie business lost the benefit of Donald's special qualities (it seems as if it would have been a magical fit, doesn't it) when his 1964 flirtation with the film program at USC petered out, his fabulous powers were reserved for greater things. Rent-collecting or building for ordinary people was not to be.

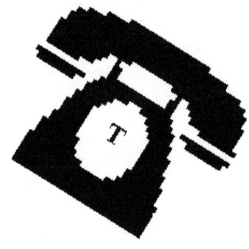

A Value-of-Dead-Wildlife Update!!

❊❊❊❊❊

THE FURS IN
IVANA'S WARDROBE
INCLUDE:

a long mink

$30,000

a shorter mink

$15,000

a full-length
chinchilla

$80,000

a red fox

$15,000
———————

TOTAL   **$140,000**

6.

TrumpCalls!   Fill in the TrumpBlank!

A. On April 4, 1990, when one phones the Trump Tower at 212 832-2000 and asks for "The Donald," the operator says:_____
a. "Is this an attorney?"
b. "May I ask who's calling?"
c. "Why?"
d. "Who?"

B. On April 4, 1990, when one phones the Trump Tower at 212 832-2000 and asks for "Marla Maples," the operator says :_____
a. "Is this an attorney?"
b. "May I ask who's calling?"
c. "Why?"
d. "Who?"

C. On April 4, 1990, when one phones the Trump Tower at 212 832-2000 and asks for "Bert Convey," the operator says :_____
a. "Is this an attorney?"
b. "May I ask who's calling?"
c. "Why?"
d. "Who?"

Answer #6:   A-b. "May I ask who's calling?"   B-c. "Why?"   C-d. "Who?" [10 points for each correct answer; 0 points for each wrong answer] _____ points earned. _____ running total.

#1. Question: Just how busy is TD?

Answer: He's so busy he just doesn't have time to run for president! Now that's busy.
And we all would so love to have him drop everything and do just that. He'd get the homeless
off the streets and into those empty apartments in rent-controlled buildings and pretty soon
there'd be lots more empty rent-controlled apartments for more homeless. For a while, anyhow.
Better to have lived in and lost a nice apartment with a million-dollar view than never to have . . .
(Can this be the beginning of a citizens' campaign?)

#2. Condominiums in Trump Place on Manhattan's Upper East Side sell for $1,000 a square foot. Thus, note the cost of setting the following items on the floor:

• bedroom slippers (like next to your bed)	$900
• one hardcover copy of *The Art of the Deal*	$870
• a chessboard	$1,180
• this book	$825
• set of skis, like Ivana might use	$3,280
• standard potato peeler	$63
• size 38 underwear (men's jockey style)	$523
• size 38 underwear (men's boxer)	$658
• one 102-page issue, *Spy* magazine	$979

A TrumpChoice!

Question: Of all of the thousands of taste choices he has had to make, what was Mr. Donald Trump's finest aesthetic decision?

Answer: Not posing nude for *Cosmopolitan*.

A TrumpAssumption!

"I'm a representative of the American people."

—The Donald, on inviting Mikhail Gorbachev over for dinner

7. IvanaTrumpQuotes
—which of the following *is* or *is not* an IvanaTrumpQuote?

		Is Not	Is So
A.	"Italy is short one mountain now because I bought all the marble I could get—twenty-five hundred tons of it." [on the Trump Tower's pink marble lobby]	___	___
B.	"Fantastic!" [on the uniforms she designed for the New Jersey Generals' cheerleaders]	___	___
C.	"I never said I was a member of the Hungarian Olympic Rolling Skating Squad!!" [in response to confusion surrounding her reported Olympic duties]	___	___
D.	"Most feminists aren't married, and have no children....They're never going to get married because they can't find a husband....I'm a normal woman."	___	___
E.	"Cowboys? We don't want Cowboys! Where can we go with Cowboys?" [on why The Donald did not buy the Dallas Cowboys]	___	___
F.	"We're young and we need the money to build and do more." [on why the Trumps don't give more money to the needy]	___	___
G.	"You'd be surprised how much it costs to look this cheap."	___	___

Answer #7: A-Is So   B-Is So   C-Is Not   D-Is Not   E-Is So   F-Is So   G-Is Not
[10 points for each correct answer; 0 points for each wrong answer; 5 bonus points if you got all of them correct!] _____ points earned. _____ running total.

We're proud to be bringing you this exclusive feature. No other feature is like this, this is the best, it's fabulous, and it is exclusive here because you deserve it. Following (from Question 8 to Question 24) is a series of questions, problems, and situations that each of us may face in our lives. How would you answer the questions— like a mensch or a short-fingered vulgarian (SFV)? (We have no idea what SFV means and we don't even know how to find out, but it has a certain ring, doesn't it?) In any case, we like to think that the answers we have chosen are the answers Mr. Donald Trump himself would choose.

8. You have just met a ravishing—to your taste—woman. She is near-blonde, athletic, personable, and speaks with some kind of accent. You think you want to marry her and spend the rest of your life with her making music together and picking out flocked wallpapers of the very best kinds. What is the first thing you do?

a) Propose at once and set about planning the wedding.

b) Call an agency to perform a background check, a firm familiar with skiers, models, and licensing procedures for interior decorators.

c) Have your lawyers draw a very tight and restrictive prenuptial agreement

d) Start calling around for the best deal in catering for the almost-first-class reception

9. What words in the list below seem most appropriate to the following description? Choose as many as you want. A filthy facade, a welfare-hotel-dingy lobby, a sleazy flea market on the ground floor, and derelicts in the doorways.

A. horror
B. glee
C. disdain
D. typical
E. pity
F. sorrow
G. opportunity
H. anger
I. dcal matcrial

---

points earned. _____ running total.

Answer #9: This is really where we start making the cut. Those who are true Trump material will not have shabby emotions, will not lose sleep, will not forget that life has to have its losers, too. Clearly, the only reasonable answers are B, I, and G. Look at that, it spells "BIG"—fantastic! It's in the genes, I guess. [Give yourself 5 points for each correct answer, plus another 35 points if you got all three, *but deduct 15 points for each incorrect answer!*]

points earned. _____ running total.

Answer #8: c) Have your lawyers draw a very tight and restrictive prenuptial agreement [award yourself 20 points if you chose c]. However, there is a 10-point penalty for choosing the incorrect answer to this vital question, a question that gets to the very heart of Trumpness. But we all learn from our mistakes. Or at least the really classy people do.]

TrumpProblem #1

10.

You are a kid. Your brother has a great set of wooden blocks. You have a great set of wooden blocks, too. You want to build a big building, bigger than the one you can build with just your blocks. So you convince your little brother to loan you his blocks. Your nice brother loans you his blocks and you get to build your building. How do you repay your brother?

    a) Return the blocks promptly and bring him a package of baseball cards after school on Monday.

    b) Buy your kid brother a Popsicle when the Good Humor man comes that evening.

    c) Glue all of his blocks together in *your* building.

    d) Convince him that it is in his best interest to let you keep his blocks, and then trade him something far less valuable.

Answer #10: c) If you chose d) do not deduct any points. It might well have been d). I wish it had been d), d) is so much more direct and forceful and dealish. Oh, well. [So, 10 points for c), 0 points for d), and deduct 5 points for choosing a) or b)] _____ points earned. _____ running total.

11.

You have just gotten a fantastic opportunity to buy for an incredibly cheap price the most fantastic piece of land on which you want to build the tallest building in the world in the greatest city in the world. The guy who is selling is a nice guy and you know the deal is great, so you offer a nonrefundable $250,000 as an option to buy. The guy goes for it! You don't want to expose $250,000 to loss, however, although you do want to go ahead and try to sell the world's greatest city on letting you build there. What do you do? (choose one)

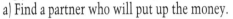

a) Find a partner who will put up the money.

b) Put the $250,000 on the barrel, because it takes money to make money.

c) Get the paperwork going and have your lawyers pick it to death so as to buy you time to sell what you don't yet own, and you still will not have put the $250,000 down.

d) Get humble and make a deal with the seller to hold the option for 96 days for $50,000 up front.

e) Walk away from it; if you can't pay, you don't play.

Answer #11: There's only one classy thing to do: stall, so c) is your answer. [If you got it right, take 10 points. Nah, make it 15. (See? The points cost us nothing but now you think we're generous guys.) If you're Merv Griffin, take 20 points.] _____ points earned. _____ running total.

★ ★ ★ E X C L U S I V E ★ ★ ★

> **A Compare-Yourself-to-Donald-Trump Breather!! TrumpFacts!! No Questions, No Answers, No Points, and No Pressure!!**

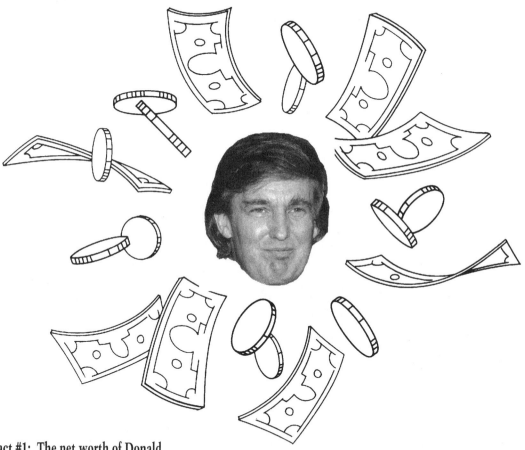

Fact #1: The net worth of Donald Trump, per pound, is $9.7 million.

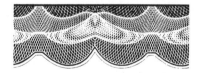

Fact #2: [An *Amazing* TrumpFact!] The Donald will not divulge the amount of cash he holds—to do so would be, he claims, "too braggadocious."

12.

You are just out of college and in Manhattan living on your own for the first time. You are meeting lots of beautiful women and are dating almost every night. But they are not satisfying. They are vain, crazy, wild, phony, incapable of normal conversation. Yet despite possessing these traits, there is something wrong with them. They are _____ and _____. (choose two of the following to fill in the blanks)

a) not morally upright
b) interested only in appearances
c) gold diggers
d) not like rocks
e) not very bright
f) too physically forward

13.

After serious soul-searching, you have concluded that your marriage is a disappointment and it has become clear that it can no longer work for you. Who are the first people you talk to about your sad decision?

a) your clergyman and closest friend
b) your children and parents
c) your public relations firm and your lawyers
d) Liz Smith and what's-her-name

Answer #12: The correct answers are b) and d); b) because appearance doesn't mean much to you at all, and d) because you are a rock and you want to be with other rocks. [20 points for each correct answer; 0 points for each wrong answer; 5 bonus points if you got both correct answers!] _____ points earned. _____ running total.

Answer #13: c) your public relations firm and your lawyers [10 points for getting this one right but dock yourself 20 if you actually chose a) your clergyman and closest friend—Geez!!] _____ points earned. _____ running total.

14.

TrumpProblem #2

When you first become aware of your own mortality, you:

a) decide to focus your energies on making every day a great one for you and your family.

b) do all those things that you always wanted to do.

c) become despondent and a little angry, but then accept it as inevitable.

d) buy a sport car and dress inappropriately.

e) take good care of yourself so that you can gracefully grow old with your spouse.

f) notice that your spouse is aging, too, and make a decision to get rid of her.

TrumpProblem # 2

points earned. _____ running total.

Answer #14: f), obviously. If you chose anything but f) you might want to consider getting a job detailing cars in a used-car lot or something of that sort. [20 points for going with f) but knock off 50 (yes, 50!) if you blew this one!]

15. TrumpProblem # 3

You are going to build a very large, tall, 20-odd-faceted building on one of the great sites in the world, replacing some garbagey old stuff. Fantastic views, Italian marble, Versailles. Real class. Now you have to find tenants. Of the profiles below, which is that of the ideal tenant?

        a) a CEO who entertains a lot and has a great art collection

        b) enlightened old money wanting to move from the cavernous old Park Avenue apartment
            to a fabulous "now" address

        c) a wealthy Italian with the beautiful wife and the red Ferrari

Answer #15: c) What else? [15 points for getting this one right, 0 points for blowing it] _____ points earned. _____ running total.

TRUMPLIGHTNINGBOLT

#1. "Listen to your gut."

#2. "Stick with what you know."

**#3. "Sometimes your best investments
are the ones you don't make."**

Besides the extraordinary originality of these TLBs, a careful reading suggests a certain Zen-like understanding of the investment field. Could it be that there is a *Zen and the Art of Not-Investing* in the TrumpFuture?)

16.

Solve the TrumpProblem

It is 1974 and building is down. New York City is in deep, deep trouble. Hey, it's your town, right? It's where you make a living and you _____ (fill in the blank with the right TrumpResponse from the list below).

a) worry about the little people.
b) work with finance and government people to get the federal government to help out.
c) see the New York crisis as a warning about greed and overexpansion and decide to be more moderate in your dealings in the future.
d) see the city's trouble as a great opportunity for yourself and think about how nice those brownstones on the West Side will look in deep, deep shadow.

17. TrumpProblem #4

You have just been to dinner with the leader of the Roman Catholic Church in the Archdiocese of New York. Besides being incredible and awesome to be taking dinner with John Cardinal O'Connor, you are in the company of his top priests! You come away with a particular view of the cardinal. Choose the right TrumpPhrase that describes that view.

a) a truly spiritual guy
b) knows how to choose a menu
c) a pretty plain dresser
d) a businessman with great political instincts
e) interesting for a celibate
f) has closets full of classy vestments

✝✝✝

Answer #17: d) a businessman with great political instincts [20 points for the right answer and if you got it wrong, give yourself 5 points anyway—they all sound "Trumpish" enough!] _____ points earned. _____ running total.

Answer #16: d) [10 points for getting this right, 0 points for getting it wrong, and 5 bonus points if you sincerely appreciated our skipping the smart-assed commentary on the answer this time.] _____ points earned. _____ running total.

18.

While your college classmates are reading the football scores and "Li'l Abner," you are: (choose only one)

a) boning up on actuarial tables.
b) practicing that special insouciance of a Friday-night singer in a New Jersey club.
c) working on a paper to knock the socks off your history prof.
d) checking the FHA foreclosure lists.
e) seeking spiritual counsel in difficult times.
f) attending debates on the troubling war in Vietnam.

A Priceless TrumpQuote!

"The point is that despite what some people may think, I'm not looking to be a bad guy when it isn't absolutely necessary."

Answer #18: You can get fantastic deals while the world burns up and the jokers watch their games; d) is hands-down right. [20 points for the right answer but 5 penalty points for this "hands-down" sort of situation!] _____

_____ points earned. _____ running total.

19. TrumpProblem #5

You have just bought a modest little boat, something that might seat sixty at an informal dinner with only the best people and wines. The boat, tied up in Baltimore, carries the name of the former owner's daughter. In all of the excitement of actually making the sale, the owner calls you, points out the sentimental value of the name, and half asks, half tells you that you "don't have any intention of using the name yourself, do you?" Of the following, how would you deal with this sentimental matter?

a) Tell him you wouldn't think of using his daughter's name and tell him you will have it painted out in the morning.

b) Take it under advisement, call your lawyer, your accountant, Liz Smith, and what's-her-name.

c) Tell the man you would never give your daughter such a terrible name.

d) Indicate that it just so happens that you had planned to use the name and that it was, in fact, very important to you. You then negotiate about a million-dollar knockdown on the price, after which the man is free to use his own daughter's name.

TrumpConsistency!
"I'm talking about the lowlifes, the horror shows for whom nothing counts but the signed contract."
--The Donald

Answer #19: d) After all, the guy signed the contract, right? [20 points for the correct answer; 0 points for blowing it.] ____ points earned. ____ running total.

★ ★ ★ E X C L U S I V E ★ ★ ★

> **Phew!—A Compare-Yourself-to-Donald-Trump Breather!!**
> **No Questions, No Answers, No Points, and No Pressure!!**

A "Hey, Louis XIV, get a load of this!" Mini-Feature!!

"There has never been anything like this built in 400 years."—The Donald, on his Trump Tower penthouse

TrumpSurvey!

At Ruthie's Diner outside of Ligonier (Pa.), an informal survey on March 15, 1990, reveals that 100 percent of the men there for the Thursday-night "spaghetti and meatball special" would gladly dump their wives if they only had to shell out 1.5 percent of their total worth.

20.

How much is it supposedly worth to you to have your name put on a publicly owned building?

a) Don't be absurd. A municipal building? That sort of thing is really vulgar, the kind of thing a classy guy wouldn't do.

b) $833,000.

c) I would only have my name on a building if it was the popular wish.

21

. What is most likely to move you to want to house the homeless?

a) I am blessed and I feel I should share my blessings with the less fortunate.

b) The deep spiritual values learned at home and from a great positive-thinking pastor.

c) Well, I'm having trouble with these tenants in rent-controlled apartments, you see, so I figure if I fill up some of the empty apartments in the building with the less decorous...(And I get to write it off!)

d) As Mother Teresa or somebody said, we are all our brother's keepers.

Answer #21: c) is the only reasonable answer. Think about it. You have just bought an apartment building overlooking a fantastic park in the world's greatest city. You discover there are people living in the apartments *who are paying reasonable rents!! People have a right to live*, you concede, but these are million-dollar views! These are views for the wealthy. These are views for which people should pay through the nose! So, you see...[20 points for choosing c), -5 points for any other choice.] _____ points earned. _____ running total.

Answer #20: b) $833,000. [30 points for choosing the correct answer *but deduct 10 points if you hesitated!*] _____ points earned. _____ running total.

22.

You have just gotten the best preparation for deal-making at Wharton and you are in love with Manhattan. You want to possess Manhattan. But you are no dummy; you know you have to get "in" with the right crowd (but not necessarily The Right Crowd, if you know what we mean) and figure that it would be very useful to become a "club man." Which of the following descriptions might best suit the club you choose to join?

a) A club in the quiet West 40s, perhaps, a little musty, a place where overt deal-making is verboten.

b) One where the intellectual stimulation comes first, and where you will rub up against first-class minds and some solid old money.

c) A place where you can get away from the daily pressures of business, where honest food, dim lights, a nice wine list, and an occasional evening of chamber music will help your spirits; and where there will be a lot of old New York money that could prove helpful.

d) The sort of place where you might see a septuagenarian with deep pockets and three Swedish blonde bombs on his arm; kind of like Studio 54 at its height.

e) An overtly business-oriented club where nobody has any pretensions to the contrary.

Answer #22: d) That's where you will find the classy guys with deep pockets and taste like your own. [20 points if you aced this one, 0 points if you blew it, and 50 bonus points if you go ahead and cancel your Rotary Club membership] _____ points earned. _____ running total.

23.

Of the following, whom do you admire?
- a) Barbara Walters
- b) Ivan Boesky
- c) Roy Cohn
- d) Michael Milken
- e) Martin Davis (NOT Marvin Davis)

24.

Which of the following film femmes would be your ideal to take up with in a clandestine relationship?

- a) a beautiful, 1949-Cadillac-convertible-driving socialite with a rich heritage and raven hair who drives you to kill your pregnant girlfriend
- b) a busty, peasant-bloused blonde in danger from Mighty Joe Young
- c) a quiet, classical, and prepossessed foreign-born beauty in danger from the Nazis in German-occupied French territory
- d) a female who gets crushed to death by a truckload of watermelons
- e) a virginal young French lady with terminal décolletage who faints with unspent passion

NOTE: This marks the end of the EXCLUSIVE Compare Yourself to Donald Trump Feature. You may proceed with the remainder of *The Really, Really Classy Donald Trump Quiz Book*, but only at your own risk.

Answer #24: d). By the way, we'd skip the fruit salad the next couple of lunches....(a) is Elizabeth Taylor, b) Terry Moore, c) Ingrid Bergman, d) Marla Maples, and e) Meg Tilley) [correct, 10 points, wrong, 0 points.] _____ points earned. _____ running total.

Answer #23: All of them!! [For each name left out of your TrumpAdmiration list, deduct 5 points. Keep trying. Keep reading. One day you'll get it right. If you didn't choose any of the names on the list, you are probably a loser with a dirty car and should set aside this book. (Do not pass it on to a friend—make your friend buy his own!)] _____ points earned. _____ running total.

LUST

25.

Of the following, only *one* is a TrumpQuote. Find it!!

A. "I can do anything. In *GQ*, I appeared as a man."
B. "Remember, wherever you go, there you are."
C. "The capacity to admire others is not my most fully developed trait."
D. "When I build something for somebody, I always add $50 million or $60 million onto the price. My guys come in, they say it's going to cost $75 million. I say it's going to cost $125 million, and I build it for $100 million. Basically, I did a lousy job. But they think I did a great job."
E. "Gertrude Stein and me are just like brothers...."
F. "In my heart, I've lusted for other women."
G. "The Holocaust was an obscene period in our nation's history. I mean this century's history. But we all lived in this century. I didn't live in this century."

points earned. —— running total

Answer #25: D. [10 points for picking D), 0 penalty points, being that you're still recovering from the Exclusive Compare Yourself to Donald Trump Feature.]

TrumpGoodwill!!

According to The Donald, by his driving up the cost of Manhattan apartments, he good-naturedly helps New York City's other boroughs because "Brooklyn and Queens and the Bronx were rotting, but now reasonably affluent people who can't afford Manhattan are moving out...."

THE TOP 13 GREATEST
TRUMPDECLARATIVESENTENCES

13. "I finally found a plane."
12. "I sensed an opportunity."
11. "There may be no other apartment like it in the world."
10. "I don't do it for money."
 9. "Sometimes—not often, but sometimes—less is more."
 8. "I always take calls from my kids...."
 7. "As long as they want to shoot, I'll shovel."
 6. "Contrary to what people think, I don't enjoy doing press."
 5. "I happen to like earth tones."
 4. "I want the best, whatever it takes."
 3. "I do it to do it."
 2. "So I ordered my guys to pull them down."

And the #1 Greatest TrumpDeclarativeSentence of Them All

1. "Don't get me wrong."

26.

What one TrumpThing does not have one or more TrumpWaterfalls in or on it?!?

A. Trump Tower—lobby
B. Trump Tower—the Trump Triplex
C. Trump's Grand Hyatt
D. Trump Tower—roof
E. *Trump Princess*
F. Trump Shuttle

When Marla shows up

in their lives, the

Trumps

bow out of

a Revlon "unforget-

table couple" adver-

tisement.

27.

Fill in the TrumpBlank in this TrumpQuote:
"We're turning the entire roof of the Trump Tower into a private park for our children. It's going to have _____

A. swings, seesaws, sandboxes,
   and a basketball court."
B. statues, waterfalls, gazebos,
   and everything else we can think of."

Answer #27: B. statues, waterfalls, gazebos, and everything else we can think of." [correct, 10 points; wrong, 0 points] _____ points earned. _____ running total.

Answer #26: F. Trump Shuttle [correct, 10 points; wrong, 0 points.] _____ points earned. _____ running total.

TRUMPLIGHTNINGBOLT

#3) "It's a lot better to side with a winner than a loser."

#1) "Sheer persistence is the difference between success and failure."

#4) "Hire the best from the best."

#2) "If you're going to make a deal of any significance, you're going to have to go to the top."

28.

Fill in the TrumpBlank!! After The Donald and Ivana split, Liz Smith began referring to him as _____

A "Old what's-his-name."
B. "The Lip."
C. "Big Boy."
D. "Lover Boy."
E. "Swivel Hips."
F. "The Other Trump."

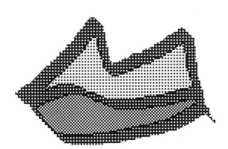

29.

After the Trumps bought their Greenwich, Connecticut, weekend mansion, they would show up _____ then go _____

A. in either a stretch limo or red convertible (with an IVANA license plate) [then go] to McDonald's.
B. in tuxedos embossed with a gold "T" [then go] to the local stock car races.
C. with friends and business associates [then go] bar-hopping.

Merry Christmas!!

The Trumps officially

update their

prenuptial agreement

on

Christmas Eve, 1987.

Answer #29: A. in either a stretch limo or red convertible (with an IVANA license plate) [then go] to McDonald's. [correct, 10 points, wrong, 0 points.] _____ points earned. _____ running total.

Answer #28: A. "Old what's-his-name" [correct, 10 points, wrong, 0 points.] _____ points earned. _____ running total.

XLIX

Great TrumpDeals from Abroad!

Over in Sydney, Australia, Ivana's ex-husband is selling his memories at the rate of $10,000 per tabloid run.

30.

Marital Experts! Match the ExpertQuote with the ExpertSource!! (Be careful—watch out for the extra ExpertSources!!)

ExpertQuote

1. "The Trump marriage is made in upper management, if not heaven."
2. "If Donald was married to a lady who didn't work and make certain contributions, he would be gone."
3. "Disregard the gossip you hear, like that Donald has a duplex reserved at Trump Tower in case the marriage falls apart; Donald and Ivana are an effective team. There is a lot of togetherness here....."
4. "He's pussywhipped in a major way. It's a marriage of convenience, but it'll go on that way."
5. "What attracts us so much together is not only the love and all that stuff, it's the energy."
6. "Rumors of marital discord in the Trump household seemed to be greatly exaggerated...."

ExpertSource

A. *New York* magazine
B. anonymous Trump employee
C. *Life* magazine
D. Ivana
E. Trump biographer Jerome Tuccille
F. Ed Koch
G. Liz Smith
H. *The New Yorker*
I. Mrs. Donald Trump

Answer #30: 1-C 2-D or I 3-A 4-B 5-D or I 6-E [10 points for each correct answer, 0 points for each wrong answer; 40 bonus points if you got all 6 correct!]

_____ points earned. _____ running total.

L

31.

Which one of the following Atlantic City quotes is bogus?!?!

1. "The cold winds blow from October to February."—Marvin Roffman (securities analyst whom Trump got fired for, in part, saying this about Atlantic City)

2. "The winter of 1980 had been particularly harsh—freezing cold and so windy that in January and February you could barely stand up on the Boardwalk."—Donald Trump (who got Marvin Roffman fired, in part, for Marvin's also including October, November, and December)

3. "The casino owners built the casinos to be self-contained entities. You can drink, you can eat, you can sleep, you can gamble right there. That was no accident; that was by design. All of our local restaurants have had to close. The casino owners destroyed the city."—Harold Mosee (former city councilor and resident of Atlantic City, the city about which Marvin Roffman said "ugly" things, which, therefore, logically, caused nonresident Trump to demand an apology)

4. "The curtain rises on a vast primitive wasteland, not unlike certain parts of New Jersey."—Woody Allen (filmmaker whose attorneys, it's assumed, are on alert)

5. "You've got a lot of dope and prostitution in Atlantic City. At nighttime you've got to have two guns out there."—Atlantic City cab driver Richard Suarez (hey, the hell with an attorney when you've got two guns!)

☞

Answer #31: 6. is bogus. [10 points if you got it right, another 10 points if 2 confused you, and yet another 10 points if you feel for Art Wulf, and if you simply got this one wrong, call your attorney!] ____ points earned. ____ running total.

You-Be-the-Judge Feature, #1

"Steve Wynn's [of the Golden Nugget] got a great act. He's a smooth talker, he's perfectly manicured, and he's invariably dressed to kill in $2,000 suits and $200 silk shirts. The problem with Wynn is that he tries too hard to look perfect and a lot of people are put off by him."

—The Donald

Your photo here!

A TrumpAnnoyance!

OFF
ON

6. "When I was four my father moved the family from Atlantic City to Scranton, then three months later on to Wilkes-Barre, because he didn't think 'some honky-tonk boardwalk was any place for a Wuft.'"—Art Wuft (Art's being sued by his own attorneys for nonpayment of his divorce billings)

32. Ivana Trump has many attributes. Of the following list, which do not describe The-Ivana-according-to-The-Donald? Choose as many as you wish! Ivana is:

a) a great manager who treats her help great
b) a rock
c) respected by her employees
d) a hardball-playing bitch
e) a Leona Helmsley in the making
f) a top model in Canada
g) almost as competitive as TDT
h) history

Answer #32: The incorrect answers are d) and h). [If you made the right choices, you know your DT, so take 15 points. Deduct 10 points for each incorrect choice. For you losers, it might be useful to a look at why the incorrect entries would be impossible to impute to The Donald. Entry d) is vulgar and not worthy of a fantastic guy. Entry h) is the kind of thing you might expect from an un-rock-like womanizer who drives his wife into breast augmentation and other miracles of the surgeon's knife-and-catgut tricks and then dumps her for someone younger and with a more prominent feature. Clearly this would not be the the style of a classy guy.] _____ points earned. _____ running total.

LII

33.
According to TD, what does Van Gogh's *Irises* represent? Choose *only* one.

    a) the work of a deranged one-eared Dutchman
    b) perhaps the most successful work of this interesting post-Impressionist painter
    c) a piece of canvas with some paint on it that some janitor might walk away with
    d) nothing compared to an Andy Wyeth

34.
According to The Donald, of the following people, who is not a rock?

    a) Fred Trump
    b) Donald Trump
    c) Donald Trump's mother
    d) Ivana Trump

Answer #34: All of them are rocks, or at least each of these people was described as a rock in 1987 in T:TAOTD. The Ivana may not be a TrumpRock any longer, having been set adrift by The Donald, as of this writing. (We've never heard of a rock drifting. Have you!) [correct, 10 points; wrong, 0 points.] _____ points earned. _____ running total.

Answer #33: c) There's something about the janitorial class that just isn't right. [correct, 10 points; wrong, 0 points] _____ points earned. _____ running total.

★ TrumpAdvice

Q: What's a really good thing to do when the deal you're working on is just about to come down and the main seller is unreachable, but has left the deal in the hands of underlings?

A: Ask for something totally unreasonable. With the boss unreachable, the guy left holding the deal will be too frightened to say no and be accused of blowing it. You may just walk away with more than the seller bargained for!

TrumpFact!

On February 17, 1990, Liz Smith—who broke the news of the Donald and Ivana Trump breakup with a full-page article several days earlier—complains that the Trump story has now degenerated into nothing more than "a media circus."

35.

Prior to being appointed president of Trump Castle, which position(s) had Ivana held?

 a) ski coach (Vermont)
 b) interior decorator (licensed, New York State)
 c) designer, cheerleaders' uniforms (New Jersey)
 d) fashion model (Canada)
 e) designer, furry hats for hotel doormen (New York City)
 f) all of the above

Answer #35: f) all of the above [correct, 10 points; wrong, 0 points.] _____ points earned. _____ running total.

LIV

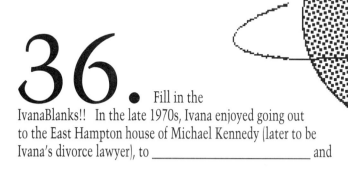

36.

Fill in the IvanaBlanks!! In the late 1970s, Ivana enjoyed going out to the East Hampton house of Michael Kennedy (later to be Ivana's divorce lawyer), to _____ and

_____

A) model clothes on the deck [and] once again experience the sensation of the modeling career from which The Donald had dragged her.

B) play her favorite Don Rickles tape [and] then repeat all the insult jokes, using The Donald's name.

C) pick blackberries [and] make her own jams.

D) study the stars [and] compose astrological charts.

You-Be-the-Judge Feature, #2

Your photo here!

"Barron Hilton is a member of what I call the Lucky Sperm Club. He was born wealthy and bred to be an aristocrat, and he is one of those guys who never had to prove anything, to anyone."

—The Donald

37.

Analyze this TrumpSentence

"I go with Ivana to look at a private school for my daughter."—The Donald

In this exercise you should think about what this means. Is he going to give his daughter to a school or give a school to his daughter? Is Ivana the child's mother or did Donald give birth to the child? What does "look" mean in the context of TrumpThought? Write an analytic essay. Send it somewhere.

Points Earned #37: Give yourself 50 points for the effort! _____ points earned. _____ running total.

A TrumpDilemma

38.

Fill-in-the-blank!! When on Larry King's show, The Donald said to the host, "Do you mind if I sit back a little? Because _____ _____

A. there's not enough room here for my ego."
B. your microphone's not picking up the proper pitch on my voice—it's a trained voice, you know?"
C. there are more caribou in this studio than you can shake a stick at."
D. your breath is very bad."
E. only the little people get this close."

The Donald is not sure whether to be happy or sad that Holiday Inns stock is standing firm in a general market sell-down. Sad, because if it declined he could buy some more cheap. Happy, because it is holding and he only stands to make many, many millions. (And you thought being Mr. Donald Trump was easy!)

Answer #38: D. your breath is very bad." [10 points if correct; 0 points and take two steps back if wrong!] _____ points earned. _____ running total.

39. The First-Ever
"Hurry-and-Catch-up-to-The-Donald" F E A T U R E

[for those under 60]—just follow the simple instructions. The simple instructions: First, list your possessions (just like The Donald's are listed!) and determine their Semi-Subtotal Value. Next, assume your current marriage or future marriage is a failure, and a judge will award 50 percent of you to your spouse (although The Donald prearranged to have his reduced by only 1 percent), and make that adjustment to your Semi-Subtotal Value to determine your Somewhat-Total Value.

Then double The Donald's Somewhat-Total Value (because he'll be making lots more money while you're still trying to catch up) while dividing your Somewhat-Total Value by 2 (because unlike The Donald, you won't have any tax abatements). This determines the Grand Totals.

Then subtract your current age from 60, and divide that number into the difference between your Grand Total and The Donald's Grand Total, then divide that by 365, then again by 16 and that's how much money you've got to make every waking hour of the rest of your working life just to catch up to Donald.

☞ Note: Mr. Art Wuft has already done his as an example.

TRUMPTHINGS		WUFTTHINGS		(Your name)THINGS	
Trump Tower	$ 155,000,000	Wuft Trailer Home	$ 16,000	___ ____	$ ____
Trump Plaza of West Palm Beach	$ 45,000,000	Wuft Dodge Dart	$ 650	___ ____	$ ____
Trump's Castle	$ 465,000,000	Wuft Elvis Memorabilia	$ 60	___ ____	$ ____
Trump Plaza (Atlantic City)	$ 560,000,000	Wuft Furnishings	$ 900	___ ____	$ ____
undeveloped sites	$ 800,000,000	Wuft Backyard	$ 725	___ ____	$ ____
Trump Management	$ 400,000,000	Wuft Huntin' Guns	$ 280	___ ____	$ ____
cash-on-hand	$ 550,000,000	cash-on-hand	$ 8	___ ____	$ ____
Trump Parc	$ 25,000,000	Wuft Dentures	$ 75	___ ____	$ ____

St. Moritz	$ 180,000,000	Wuft Beer Cooler	$ 15	___ ___		$ ___	
Trump Enter-prises	$ 130,000,000	Wuft Bowling Ball	$ 25	___ ___		$ ___	
Grand Hyatt	$ 165,000,00	Wuft Velvet Art	$ 17	___ ___		$ ___	
Trump Plaza	$ 260,000,000	___ ___	$ —	___ ___		$ ___	
Trump Plaza (of New York City)	$ 20,000,000	___ ___	$ —	___ ___		$ ___	
Trump Palace	$ 70,000,000	___ ___	$ —	___ ___		$ ___	
Trump Air	$ 365,000,000	___ ___	$ —	___ ___		$ ___	
	▬▬▬▬		▬▬▬▬			▬▬▬▬	
Semi-Subtotal Value	$4,190,000,000		$18,755			$___	
(minus 1%)	− 41,900,000	(minus 50%)	− 9,378	(minus 50%)		−___	
	▬▬▬▬		▬▬▬▬			▬▬▬▬	
Somewhat-Total Value •	$4,148,100,000 x 2 ☞		$ 9,377 $ ÷ 2 ☞			___ ÷ 2 ☞	

Grand Total	$8,296,200,000	$ 4,689	$____
		$8,296,200,000 – $4,689	$8,296,200,000 – $
Grand Total Difference		$8,296,195,311	$____
÷Age ratio	÷(60 – 38 = 22)	÷(60 – __ = __)
	$377,099,787	$____
÷365, then 16	÷365	÷365
	$ 1,033,153	$____
	÷16	÷16

**Money to be made
every
waking
hour
of
the
rest
of
one's
working
life
just to
catch up to
The Donald.**

$ 64,572 $_____

Points Earned #39: If you *actually completed* the First-Ever "Hurry-and-Catch-up-to-The-Donald" Feature (for those under 60), give yourself 300 points!! [for your spunky attitude and your apparent insistence on going through with this TrumpMadness . . . phew!] ____ points earned. ____ running total.

LXI

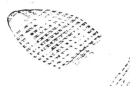
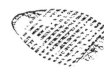

40.

While attending the Wharton School of Finance, Trump walked around campus wearing _____ (fill in the blank)

a) a Superman shirt and cape.
b) maroon suits with matching shoes.
c) plastic sandals.
d) a power ponytail.

A Complete Pair of
TrumpLightningBolts!!

#1. "Deals work best when each side gets something it wants from the other."

#2. "Pennies turn into dollars."

Answer #40: b) maroon suits with matching shoes. [correct, 10 points, wrong, 0 points.] _____ points earned. _____ running total.

LXII

Your
photo
here!

41.

When The Donald says "The Trump Taj Mahal will be beyond everything else," just what is *"everything else"*?

a. Trump Tower, Trump Plaza, Trump Parc, Trump Castle, Trump Etc.
b. Columbus (Ohio), if you're coming by way of Des Moines (Iowa)
c. generally accepted standards of good taste
d. only The Donald knows

"I'd always admired Walter

Hoving [Tiffany owner]...he

was a man with perfect

white hair, beautifully

tailored suits, and an

imperial style."

—The Donald

Answer #41: d. only The Donald knows [correct, 10 points; wrong, 0 points.]
points earned._____running total.

42.

"A Trump Descriptions" Feature!! Which of the following would best describe a Taj Mahal-like and Trump-like project?

a) A superb piece of architecture of white marble into which drawings have been incised and set with precious stones, built around a reflecting pool and walled garden. Commissioned as a fitting memorial to a woman loved.

b) A piece of ersatz architecture in a bus stop town where the cold onshore winter winds and grayness combine to depress the hell out of everybody except the few polyester-panted grandmothers who have hit it at one of the 3,000 slot machines and 267 gaming tables that, with a lot of luck and no winter, may provide a way to pay off $94.5 million annual debt service.

c) The best of everything, really fabulous, with onion domes and miles and miles of just the best carpets that can be created from oil slag. And big, I mean big, three football fields' worth of just fabulous gaming, and with hotels and helicopter pads and the best people coming and spending and having a really fabulous time. And really classy people like boxing promoters with hair problems and sports figures accused of a little wife-beating, that sort of thing, but a family kind of place, and a fitting memorial to megalomania.

d) An incredibly classy pleasure palace by the warm Jersey shore.

Answer #42: What else but d)! You know our Donald!! [Bingo! 40 points for hitting the jackpot, but if you blew it, pay the house off with 20 penalty points!] _____ points earned. _____ running total.

LXIV

THE FORMING OF

MR. DONALD TRUMP

It was hard for a young man of modest means to get a leg up in Manhattan. Here he was, a kid from the boroughs who had only known the inside of military school and Wharton the last several years. But discipline combined with great ambition and voraciousness for reading foreclosure notices would stand him in good stead. Dad helped a little, too, but as Donald would come to say, he did it on his own. Heck, what could 15,000 apartments Trump *père* had built in the boroughs possibly generate? Several millions at best.

He moved out of the Tara-columned house in Queens and on his own moved into the core of the Big Apple, a town he had his eye on for some time and whose skyline he wished to change. Before you could say, "Fifty-six into sixty-eight goes once, nothing left over," Mr. Donald Trump was getting concessions from the city, redefining the art of the deal *and* our numeric system, charming the air rights out of

Tiffany, and bashing Mayor Edward Koch like a veteran of the little island of Manhattan. Whew!

During this period, much of the Trump that we have come to know and wonder at came into being. Those loud, crazy, and vain women he met at his social club were replaced by a veritable rock, Ivana, daughter of an electrical engineer, a skier, a model, a woman with a decorating touch that is pure Ivana. The couple managed to raise three children while redesigning the Manhattan that we now know. Donald not only built the city's only 68-story building with 56 floors, got rid of the old Bonwit's and had their dumb old Art Deco details blasted to kingdom come, and made really classy new hotel lobbies with *real art* in them, but—now get this for warmth—*was always willing to take phone calls from the kids* while all this was going on. We don't know about you, but we get choked up just thinking about it.

And then he bought an airline and called it Trump, and a boat and called it Trump, and a casino and a lot of other stuff and most of them got called Trump. This was all accomplished with the full partnership of a good woman who gave up a career as a *Top* Model for Manhattan and Donald and charity work. A rock, indeed. A great couple, a great story, in a great—no, the greatest—city in the world.

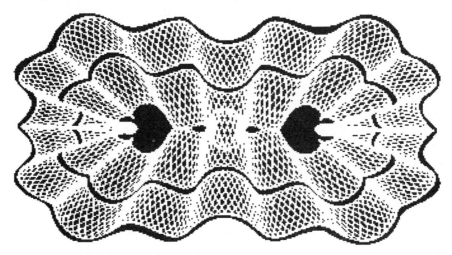

43.

"A TrumpEssay" Feature!!

Is there any connection between the fact that April 1 is April Fool's Day and also the opening date in 1990 of Mr. Donald Trump's Taj Mahal Casino and Resort on the balmy Jersey shore?

Write a speculative essay of 600-700 words. Put the essay in a bottle and cork it. Put on your parka, your gloves, your galoshes. Take the bus to Atlantic City in November. Put the bottle in the waters of the balmy Jersey shore. Cover your mouth when you sneeze.

Guess whose living room has 27 hand-carved marble columns . . . hand carved by real Italians in Italy from Italian marble!!! . . . which makes it just like Versailles, according to the apartment owner. [Enter owner's name here: _____. No answer is supplied by us, the editors. If you *need* the answer, dock yourself 100 penalty points—Geez!! If you *do not need* the answer, give yourself 50 bonus points!!]

_____ points earned.

_____ running total.

Points Earned #43: If you made it all the way to the sneeze, this bit of madness is good for 15 points [if you skipped any part of #20, don't worry, be happy!]

_____ points earned. _____ running total.

The shower in the owner's suite of the *Trump Princess* has thirteen nozzles and is carved in the shape of a scallop shell from a single piece of onyx—a task that took a team of workers a year to complete.

44.

A TrumpMatch featuring TrumpSubjects and TrumpOpinions!! Match the TrumpSubject in column A with the TrumpOpinion in column B.

A

1) Trump Tower
2) Taj Mahal Resort
3) Trump Shuttle
4) *Trump Princess*
5) Ivana Trump
6) the Plaza Hotel
7) the Trump living room
8) *Trump: The Art of the Deal*

B

a) none of those below
b) an amazing success
c) the biggest
d) a fantastic success
e) the ultimate piece of property
f) the single greatest franchise in the world
g) one of the great diamonds of the world
h) the finest piece of art on water

[correct!] _____ points earned. _____ running total.

Answer #44: 1-e) 2-d) 3-f) 4-h) 5-a) 6-g) 7-c) 8-b) [10 points for each correct answer; 0 points for each wrong answer; 5 bonus points if you got all 8

Trump Manners

45. The Donald actually shows up in Judith Krantz's novel *I'll Take Manhattan*. Using a TrumpX ("TX"), note which of the following were *penned by Krantz* and which were *mouthed by The Real Donald!!* [The first one is done for you!]

	Krantz's Donald	The Real Donald
A. "I love real estate because there's something about creating something that's visible. There's an artistic merit."	__	TX
B. "I don't want to be made anybody's sucker."	__	__
C. "Hey you, pretty girl, what's the problem."	__	__
D. "Look, it will take me a little time to make the best possible deal for you but if you want to turn the apartment over to me I'll write you a check for six million."	__	__
E. "...I don't have PR agents and I don't enjoy doing interviews...."	__	__
F. "I hate the concept of divorce. It's not nice."	__	__

Answer #45: A-The Real Donald B-The Real Donald C-Krantz's Donald D-Krantz's Donald E-The Real Donald F-The Real Donald [10 points for each correct answer, 0 points for each wrong answer, 25 bonus points if you got all 6 correct!] ____ points earned. ____ running total.

According to The Donald!

"It is very strange for a guy to be divorcing his wife while still loving her and keeping her as a good friend." [We can understand that. Can't you? It's so much better to have an acrimonious, public bloodletting, don't you agree?]

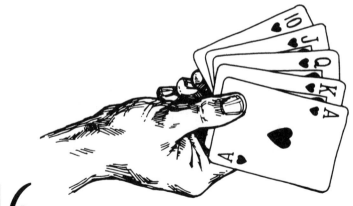

46.

Fact or Fiction!?! Put a TrumpX ("TX") in the correct column!

	Fact	Fiction
A. As owner of the New Jersey Generals, Trump signs Giants' linebacker Lawrence Taylor to a contract. Then, a couple of days later, sells the contract to the Giants for $750,000; i.e., Trump sells several sheets of paper—that hadn't existed days earlier— for $ 3/4 million.	___	___
B. Trump essentially forces the trustees of the Post Foundation to sell him Mar-a-Lago, by first buying the beach rights for $2 million and then threatening to put up a hideous building of his own at the ocean's edge.	___	___
C. The Donald likes to brag about how he let Diamond Shamrock Corporation spend all the money ($27 million) on the best private jet in the world and then, when an oil pinch hit, Trump bought it for only $8 million.	___	___
D. In 1985, The Donald sued Omar Shariff for his continuing use of the term "Trump" in his syndicated column on bridge playing.	___	___

☞

Answer #46: A-Fact B-Fact C-Fact D-Fiction E-Fact [10 points for each correct answer; 0 points for each wrong answer; 20 bonus points if you got all 5 correct.] ___ points earned. ___ running total.

E. After Trump won control of Resorts International, he persuaded the board to award him a management contract that would pay him $100 million over five years to run the company and oversee completion of the Taj. (Since completing the Taj was his principal goal in buying Resorts, it wasn't clear why he needed a $100 million inducement.) When Merv Giffin then came along and topped Trump's offer to take Resorts private, Merv agreed to pay Trump $63 million to buy out the management contract. Thus, Trump received $63 million for an agreement he cooked up as an incentive to himself to do something he wanted to do anyway, or as The Donald notes, "I will be getting $63 million for a piece of paper that didn't exist six weeks earlier."

TrumpScript!

Question: "What won't this story do, whatever the TrumpStory of the moment might be?"

The Donald: "It won't quit!"

Well, That Explains Why She Always Looks Different Than She Did the Other Time!

His entry in *Who's Who in Finance and Industry* has The Donald marrying Ivana "Zelnicek," his entry in *The International Who's Who* has him marrying Ivana "Winkelmayr," and *Life* has him married to Ivana "Zelnickova."

47.

Of the following, which is *not* a TrumpQuote?

a) "If I were starting off today I would love to be a well-educated black because I believe they do have an actual advantage."

b) "I look for things for the art sake and the beauty sake, and for the deal sake."

c) "It happens that I'm heterosexual."

d) "It's [the Trump divorce story] bigger than Elizabeth Taylor and Richard Burton."

e) "Deals are my art form."

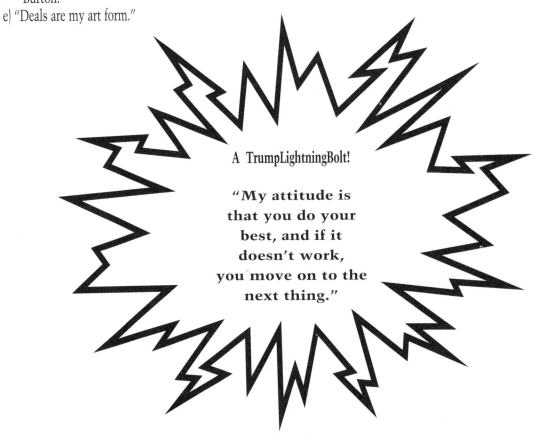

A TrumpLightningBolt!

"My attitude is that you do your best, and if it doesn't work, you move on to the next thing."

Answer #47: c) obviously is not TrumpLike. Any number of therapists have commented on the obvious phallic nature of TrumpBuildingsProjects and the aggressive heterosexuality that underlies the need to prove his virile nature through playing with "these huge Erector sets," as Dr. Maldroit calls TDT's buildings. We think that goes kind of far, don't you? [correct, 10 points; wrong, 0 points; but 10 penalty points for being sucked in by the Ed Koch quote] _____ points earned. _____ running total.

48.

A Trump Trick Question!!

What do you need to hit a real home run? (Think about this one. Remember, context is everything.) About one sentence ought to do. Enter your answer here:

_____

_____

_____

_____

Answer #48: A twenty-eight-sided building of insufferable height with two views from each room in apartments that will get the highest possible price. [10 points if you're somewhat close, and hey, what the heck, give yourself 5 points if you went with a sentence that somehow involved Hank Aaron. (My, how the game has changed!)]

_____ points earned. _____ running total.

LXXIII

TrumpFacts—Three of Them!!!

#1. In 1987, while being interviewed, standing in the middle of a room decorated with the many magazine covers on which he's appeared—like trophies from some media safari—The Donald tells *People* magazine, "I don't like publicity, I absolutely hate doing interviews."

#2. The Stage Deli Restaurant offers a Donald Trump Power Sandwich featuring Nova Scotia salmon, cream cheese, tomato, lettuce, and onions. (Must be what Larry King ate.)

#3. In Washington, D.C., a woman actually paid $2,800 to 1) bleach her brown hair, and 2) have extra human hair bonded onto her tresses to get that "Ivana Trump look."

TrumpBlah!

Q: What does a friend say The Donald doesn't like?

A: To be touched. Well, we mean, you know, not to be touched when he doesn't want to be touched. You can understand that, can't you? Like a person could just come up and touch you, you know, and that would be really creepy, don't you think? (There's nothing wrong with this, you know. It's normal. Sort of.)

49.

Put the TrumpEvents in the correct order—fill in the numbers, from 1 to 12!!

TrumpEvent	Correct Order
A. Buddied up to Don King	___
B. Left his aging wife	___
C. Hired Roy Cohn	___
D. Built a skyscraper out of toy blocks and glue	___
E. Buddied up to Ed Koch	___
F. Joined "Le Club"	___
G. Married a Czechoslovakian woman	___
I. Got sent off to military school	___
J. Buddied up to Mike Tyson and Robin Givens	___
K. Dumped all over Ed Koch	___
L. Led a military academy contingent up Fifth Avenue	___
M. Had shutters installed on lower-income housing in Cincinnati to make them look "classy"	___

___ points earned. ___ running total.

[10 points for each correct answer; 0 points for each wrong answer!]

Answer #49: 1-D 2-I 3-L 4-M 5-F 6-E 7-C 8-G 9-A 10-K 11-J 12-B

50.

True! False! or Other!! (i.e., claimed by a Trump, but the proof's lacking).

	True	False	Other
A. When someone, for example, Bert Convey, is on the 30th floor of the Trump Tower, Bert's really on the 23rd floor.	—	—	—
B. When someone, for example, Bert Convey, is on the 14th floor of Trump's Grand Hyatt (in New York City) Bert's really on the 6th floor.	—	—	—
C. Trump graduated first in his class from the University of Pennsylvania's Wharton School of Finance.	—	—	—
D. Ivana was a member of the Czechoslovakian Olympic ski team in Sapporo, Japan.	—	—	—
E. At one time, Ivana was the top model in Montreal.	—	—	—
F. The Donald led the New York Military Academy contingent in New York City's 1963 Columbus Day parade.	—	—	—

A TrumpQuote!

❝Holiday Inns and Ramada didn't have enough class.❞

Answer #50: A-True B-True C-Other D-False E-Other F-True [10 points for each correct answer; 0 points for each wrong answer; 5 bonus points if you got all 6 correct!] ____ points earned. ____ running total.

LXXVI

51.

Match the quote with the source!!

Quote

1. "Greedy."
2. "I am not a schmuck."
3. "The chicks think I'm 50."
4. "Donald Trump is the Michael Jackson of real estate."
5. "Moron. Incompetent."
6. "Anytime you call the mayor a moron, it's a terrible mistake."
7. "A man like Donald Trump comes along maybe only twice in a century."
8. "He was no Boy Scout."

Source

A. The Donald's father, Fred
B. Irving Fischer
C. The Donald, on Ed Koch
D. Ed Koch, on The Donald
E. Trump associate, on The Donald
F. The Donald, on Roy Cohn
G. Howard Rubenstein, The Donald's PR man
H. The Donald, on The Donald

TrumpInsight!

Question:

"What makes Blanche Sprague, vice-president in charge of sales, a classic?"

The Donald:

"A mouth that won't quit."

A TrumpFact!

You know how you can always tell a loser, huh? Well, you can tell a lousy no-good loser by the very fact that a crummy, no-class loser tries to sell his car when it is filthy dirty. That's how. And that's a TrumpFact.

Answer #51: 1-D 2-H 3-A 4-B 5-C 6-E 7-G 8-F [10 points for each correct answer, 0 points for each wrong answer; 20 bonus points if you got all 8 correct!] _____ points earned. _____ running total.

52.

The Donald is a Gemini, the sign of the Twins. Which of the following astrological traits is *not* a Gemini?!? Indicate your choice with a TrumpStar (T*). The first is done for you as an example.

	Is	Is Not
A. You love being around people and parties 'cause you love to talk, and you're always fun and witty.	T*	—
B. You love to confuse everyone and keep 'em guessing— that keeps you from being pinned down. But you're such a charmer that you get away with it.	—	—
C. Geminis distrust emotions. Love for them is a mental thing instead of a feeling thing, which is sometimes a shock to their mates.	—	—
D. You are a will-o-the-wisp who doesn't want to be tied down—you are clever, never dull, always stimulating and exciting.	—	—
E. You instinctively know what will please the public and how to bring this about through your clever super-sensitivity to pink marble and gurgling waterfalls.	—	—

points earned. _____ running total.

Answer #52: A-Is B-Is C-Is D-Is E-Is Not [10 points for each correct guess, 0 points for each wrong answer.]

LXXVIII

53.

This is your TrumpLife!! What was the outstanding event in the life of second-grade student Donald Trump?

a) He won the state spelling bee.
b) He discovered a new way to multiply and sold his discovery to the Board of Education.
c) He gave his teacher a black eye because he did not meet the demanding young Donald's perception of what made a good music teacher.
d) He kissed his first unrelated blonde.
e) During recess, he won all the kids' money in Three Card Monte without the help of a lookout.

#1 on The Donald's "It's About Time Someone Spoke Up" List!

"He's almost a throwback to the nineteenth century as a promoter. He's larger than life."

—Victor Palmieri, the guy who sold the West Side railroad yards to DT

Answer #53: c). He gave his teacher a black eye because he did not meet the demanding young Donald's perception of what made a good music teacher. [10 points for getting this right, if you got it wrong, pop yourself one right in the old left eye—BAM!!] _____ points earned. _____ running total.

A TrumpTiff!

"The prenuptial agreement signed by Donald and Ivana Trump is a lengthy and detailed document covering all aspects and is 100 percent enforceable in courts of law."
—**spokesperson for The Donald**

"We do not consider the so-called prenuptial agreement to be serious. It will have no relevance to a court because it is unconscionable and fraudulent."
—**spokesperson for The Ivana**

54.

The Trump-the-Critic Feature!!—which *one* of the following is *not* a TrumpQuote?!?

A. "I'm only interested in Old Masters."

B. "Contemporary art is a con."

C. "The *Trump Princess* is the greatest piece of art on water. It's the *Mona Lisa*. It's a major masterpiece."

D. "For me this is like owning the *Mona Lisa*. It's not just an investment, it's a work of art." [on the Plaza]

E. "Art, like morality, consists of drawing the line somewhere."

F. "It's junk!" [on the Bonwit building's Art Deco frieze]

G. "The classical elements in postmodern designs almost always look imitative."

H. "I'd never been a big fan of postmodernism. . . . "

Answer #54: E. "Art, like morality, consists of drawing the line somewhere." [10 points if correct, 5 penalty points if you went with B or C] _____ points earned. _____ running total.

LXXX

55.

Who said the following?

"... the Taj Mahal will come off as Atlantic City with the volume turned up...."

    a) Donald Trump
    b) Malcolm Forbes
    c) Johnny Carson
    d) some writer characterized as wearing cheap suits
    e). Ivana Trump
    f) architect Francis X. Dumont (who?)

Another Trump Sentence to Analyze!

Mr. Donald Trump donated his royalties from T:TAOTD to charity. Terence Paré quotes Donald Trump in *Fortune* as saying the following about the prospects (now happily upon us) of writing another book:

> **"If I can give $4 million or $5 million to charity because I decide to write a book, I may have that obligation to myself."**

In his saying that he may have that obligation *"to myself,"* some have wondered if the act of giving, that which is going outward, has become in the end, self-referential, that is, coming back to the self. Some of those who have wondered think that it was an error of spoken English or it was "misspoken." Other think, as others invariably will, that some sort of selfish tax or promotional concern was at work. Think about it. Put together a discussion group. Write us with your thoughts. Or maybe, better yet, you would like to write to Mr. Donald Trump with your thoughts.

Answer #55: d) None other than Paul Goldberger of the *New York Times*. For those of you who have been napping, Mr. Dumont is the architect of the fabulous Taj. He also is noted for his use of the ironic column. [10 points if correct, but 5 penalty points if you went with b]—he's dead!] _____ points earned. _____ running total.

56.

Who's saying what about The Donald! Match the source with the quote!

1. "Cary Grant had his accent; Clark Gable his pencil mustache. Donald Trump has his money and power, and like the other romantic heroes, he knows what to do with them."
2. "The man has flair...."
3. "Donald Trump is a deal maker. He is a deal maker the way lions are carnivores and water is wet."
4. "America's most glamorous young tycoon...."
5. "Trump's life is dramatic proof that the rewards are there for those who dare."
6. "A no-nonsense comer ... big-time real estate tycoon ... master wheeler-dealer and consummate real estate entrepreneur...."
7. "... Brilliant entreprencur. Donald Trump is blunt, brash, surprisingly old-fashioned ... and always an original."
8. "He is in some ways the ultimate wanna-be...."
9. "He gave his name to a board game, an airline, a middle-European model and skier, and practically an era; the man who saved pink marble from being relegated to bathrooms by Billy Baldwin."

A. *New York Times Times Book Review*
B. *Fortune*
C. *Chicago Sun-Times*
D. *San Antonio Express and News*
E. *San Diego Union*
F. *Virginia-Pilot and Ledger-Star*
G. *Milwaukee Journal*
H. *Berkshire Eagle*
I. editors, *The Really, Really Classy Donald Trump Quiz Book*

Answer #56: 1-C 2-A 3-E 4-D 5-H 6-F 7-G 8-B 9-I [10 points for each correct answer; 0 points for each wrong answer, but 25 bonus points for getting entry 9 correct!] _____ points earned. _____ running total.

LXXXII

57.

Which of the following descriptions best fits what Mr. Donald Trump said, in November of 1989, was going to be "a tremendous success"?

a) A casino that opens just as casino profits are falling.
b) A business started in part with $675 million in junk bonds which cost $94.5 million a year just in interest.
c) A resort built in the northeast where it's cold and snowy from October to April.
d) A business that analyst Marvin Roffman says is not recession-proof.

A SUPER
TrumpLightningBolt!!

"Hey, life is life."

"We have to buy a lot of books. I really respect books."
—The Donald, on the empty library shelves of his renovated Trump Tower penthouse

Answer #57: a), b), c), and d) [correct, 10 points; wrong, 0 points.] _____ points earned. _____ running total.

TrumpFacts!!

1. Texts drawls make Donald Trump feel very comfortable. (Isn't that something!)

2. The fact that oil in oil wells is underground makes Donald Trump uncomfortable. (We can understand that, can't you?)

58. Fill in the blanks. Among the owners of Trump condos and co-ops are: Johnny Carson, Liberace (past owner), _____, Martina Navratilova, _____, Governor John Brown, Sophia Loren, David Merrick, Steven Spielberg, _____, and Morton Downey.

a) Ed Koch, Merv Griffin, Bert Convey
b) Phyllis George, Paul Anka, Dick Clark
c) Liz Smith, Don Shula, Bryant Gumbel
d) Sylvester Stallone, Tom Cruise, Mrs. Bonnechelli

Answer #58: b) Phyllis George, Paul Anka, Dick Clark [correct, 10 points; wrong, 0 points.] _____ points earned. _____ running total.

LXXXIV

59. THE "HOW'S YOUR DOMESTIC LIFE COMPARED TO THE DONALD'S"

HARDLY-SCIENTIFIC-BUT-VERY-CLASSY SURVEY!

SCORE/POINTS
(circle the correct number of points and total at the end)

Your age [supposedly]:

• 20-35	20 points
• 36-45	80
• 46-55	20
• 56+	0

Your sex: • male | 100

• female [if so, this is going to be real tough for you!]	1

Your education:

• public elementary, middle, and high schools	10
• military academy, Fordham University, and the Wharton School of Finance, University of Pennsylvania [note: that's Ivy League!]	92

Percentage of your possessions named after yourself [for example, if you're Bert Convey, you might have possessions such as The ConveySofa, The ConveyRefrigerator, The ConveySquashRacket, The ConveySnowShovel, etc.]:

• 90 to 100%	90
• 50 to 89%	70
• 1 to 22%	10
• 0%	0

Your annual income:

• less than $20,000	0
• $20,000 to $100,000	10
• $100,000 to $1 million	20
• $1 million to $10 million	30
• $11 million to $50 million	70
• $50 million +	99

Rate your wife as an Alpine downhill skier:

• can barely stand	10
• slaloms like Mel Torme	20
• looks damn good in the lodge	70
• Liz Smith even calls her "coach"	80
• good enough to catch the eye of a wild and crazy American stud	90

Favorite place to meet new women:

• local computerized dating service	7
• your own yacht	50

• your own hotel	50
• your own casino	50
• in church, preferably the one in which you married your current wife	90

Is it your spouse's first marriage?

• yes	11
• no	21
• maybe	91

Do you have children?

• yes	50
• no	10

Bonus Opportunity!—If yes, do you make business calls while bathing with them?

• yes	120!
• no	0

Rate of hair spray usage:

• none	3
• minimal	4
• average	5
• incredibly excessive	93

Whom do you buddy around with?

• Don King, Jack Nicolson, Mike Tyson, Don Johnson, Barbara Walters, Doug Flutie, Prince Charles, and Abe Rosenthal	91
• my neighbor, Herb; my brother, Wally; and sometimes, a couple of the guys from the bowling league	7

Complete this sentence: I feel closest to my spouse when we are

• making love.	20

- making money.   99
- making hot dogs and beans.   2
- making the news.   97

Do you and your spouse have pet names for each other?
- yes   92
- no   17

Bonus Opportunity!—If you do, is the pet name preceded by "The,"   120!
like in "The Donald" or, if you happened to be Bert Convey, "The Bert"?

What's your pet name for your favorite gossip columnist?
- The Mouth   71
- Hips Smith   80
- Honeybuns   95

Accessibility of your underwear to the general public:
- minimal   3
- just my wife and the guys   4
  down at the racquet club
- family only   92

If I met my ex-wife, who's now worth $25 million, tomorrow, I would marry her all over again.
(circle one and enter that number as this question's points on the blank provided)

| 10 | 20 | 30 | 40 | 50 | ___ |
| agree | | | | disagree | |

My best friend is:
- my wife   4
- my father   80
- William Zeckendorf   99

If I could change anything about my spouse,
it would be (check all that apply):

• her lips	82
• her annoying fear of gas stoves	91
• her breasts	95
• her annoying fear of gas heat	91
• her tendency to ski on the same slope as my mistress	98
• her annoying fear of gas water heaters	91
• her Winnebago	22
• her accent	87
• that she *wasn't* a top model	89
• her sexual performance	77
• her salary	90
• her personal habits	85
• her mother	94
• her lack of humor	24
• her hair	98
• that she did *not* ski at Sapporo	89
• the color of her nail polish	81
• her married name	69
• her wardrobe—more T-shirts!	53

If you had a mistress, would you:

• find her a nice hotel room	3
• buy her a Winnebago	14
• stash her in the apartment downstairs	97

Most of the arguments we have are about:

• marble	92
• who lives downstairs	97
• naming things	90
• philosophy, art, and theology	7
• her salary	82
• my lower lip	88
• clothing	61
• her looks	89
• waterfalls	92
• her sexual performance	89

What my spouse doesn't know about me is generally in the area of my (check all that apply):

• academic record	22
• sex life	94
• fantasies	53
• military career	21
• hair	89

TOTAL POINTS _____

If you scored **less than 500**, "you're no Donald" and should therefore immediately forget about that Eastern European mail-order bride offer.

If you scored **2000 or higher,** "CONGRATULATIONS!— you're Donald material" and should therefore 1) dump your wife, and 2) commence suing anybody with your name (for example, if you're Bert Convey, sue the hell out of that Bert guy on *Sesame Street*).

☛ **Note:** If you scored **between 500 and 2000,** you've got serious psycho-identification problems; i.e., you're confused, you're neither here nor there, nutzo, your act's falling apart, you don't know if you're coming or going. So if you're in a marriage, get out of it! If you're not, stay put!

☛ **Note: BE SURE TO INCLUDE THESE "HOW'S YOUR DOMESTIC LIFE COMPARED TO THE DONALD'S" POINTS IN YOUR GRAND TOTAL!!.**

_____ running total.

60.

"The Trump Line" (a 900 phone number costing $1.49/minute) provides the latest "previously unreported information" and developments "as they happen" on the "billionaire boy wonder" and the women in his life. Which of the following developments *was never actually offered?*

	Was	Was Not
A. A re-created phone conversation between The Donald and Marla Maples which features tidbits of conversation like "Hi, honey, are you busy?"	—	—
B. An "explosive interview" with "super sexy French model Chantal DePeyrac," who reveals her "romantic interludes" with The Donald.	—	—
C. Details on how running back Herschel Walker "masterminded the game plan" and introduced The Donald and The Marla.	—	—
D. Revealing information about The Donald's "odd habits and obsessions," like how some consider him arrogant and that he's come close to phoning Fidel Castro and George Bush just to say what's on his mind.	—	—
E. The "first time ever revelations surrounding the secret ingredients" of the recipe for "Trump Treats: The Caramel Popcorn."	—	—
F. "Hot details surrounding the Donald Trump/Brigitte Neilsen/Sylvester Stallone love triangle."	—	—

Answer #60: A, B, C, D, and F-Was E-Was Not [10 points for each correct answer; 0 points for each wrong answer.] _____ points earned. _____ running total.

XCI

TrumpChores— Phew!!

Ivana likes to tell how she did her Christmas shopping. The nanny took her three children through F.A.O. Schwartz and rated their expression of joy, writing the toy numbers and prices. Then Ivana called, the gifts were wrapped, the driver picked them up, and as she dusts her hands against each other, Ivana exclaims, "Bing! Bong! Done!"

61.
TrumpStars! Match The Donald's horoscope with the event and the date on which it occurred.

Event and Its Date

1) June 14, 1946: Birth of The Donald.

2) February 3, 1972: The Winter Olympics open in Sapporo, Japan, and many attend including alternates of the Czechoslovakian downhill ski team.

3) November 6, 1973: Abe Beame is elected mayor of New York City.

4) April 9, 1977: The marriage of Ivana and The Donald.

5) March 26, 1990: Ivana's attorneys file papers in New York State Supreme Court seeking 50 percent of The Donald's $5 billion.

6) April 1, 1990: The Taj Mahal opens.

The Donald's Horoscope on that Day

a) In commercial matters, don't let your emotions override your logic and common sense. Placating your feelings could prove to be unprofitable.

b) Bold measures may be required to overcome a static development. However, your moves must be well thought out.

c) Partnership arrangements could fall short of their mark if those involved are not good team players.

d) This should be a very productive day for you.

_____ points earned. _____ running total.

Answer #61: 1-b)   2-c)   3-d)   4-e)   5-a)   6-f)   [10 points for each correct answer; 0 points for each wrong answer; 25 bonus points if you got all 6 correct!]

e) Unless you are well disciplined and budget minded, there is a possibility you might spend more than you intend.

f) Even though you're a good salesperson, others will be able to see through your ploys.

62

More IvanaTrumpQuotes! Which of the following *is* or *is not* an IvanaTrumpQuote?!?

	Is Not	Is So
A. "There is no wallpaper, no fabric, no lacquer, no carpet, no marble in any of our buildings that didn't get my approval . . . then, of course, I bring it to my husband for *his* approval."	——	——
B. "I know what I like."	——	——
C. "Of course, we don't *have* too many houseguests, since we own a few hotels around town."	——	——
D. "I never intend to look a day over 28, but it's going to cost Donald a bundle."	——	——
E. "Women who stay home with their children, just stare at the ceiling!"	——	——
F. "We're young and we need the money to build and do more." [on why the Trumps don't give more money to the needy]	——	——
G. "You'd be shocked at how much it costs to look this cheap."	——	——

A TrumpQuote

"You can be happy on a lot less money."

—The Donald, on Michael Milken's annual salary of $550,000

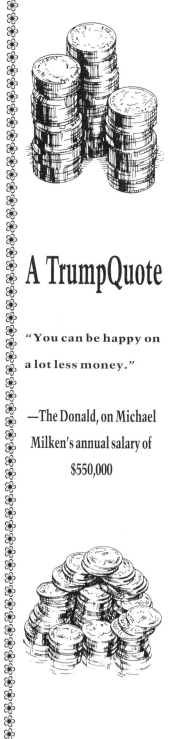

Answer #62: A, B, C, D, E, and F-is So, G-is Not [10 points for each correct answer; 0 points for each wrong answer; 25 bonus points if you got all 7 correct!]

_____ points earned. _____ running total.

A TrumpQuote!

"I can be very happy living in a one bed-room apartment, believe me."

TrumpQ&A

Question: What must be very reassuring to Donald Trump when he is working in his office and feels tired, discouraged, at the low ebb of his energies?

Answer: To be able to look up and see himself reflected in his gold-glass-tile ceiling, don't you think?

63. Which of the following are the published quotes of TrumpFriends attempting to explain the enigmatic Mr. Donald Trump?

a) "A black hole in space."

b) "What he wants still is acceptance from his father. He is playing out his insecurities on an incredibly large canvas."

c) "He had more fun screwing Merv Griffin than he ever did having sex with a woman."

d) "He's so exclusively involved with himself . . . there's no room for another person."

e) "He's obsessive-compulsive."

A TrumpLightningBolt!
"I'm not the happiest person."

Answer #63: All of them—a), b), c), d), and e). What are friends for? [10 points for each correct answer; 0 points for each wrong answer; 15 bonus points if you got all 5 correct.] _____ points earned. _____ running total.

64.

Who are the slender and dreamy, even dweebish [sic] young millionaires on the following list?

      a) Steven Spielberg
      b) Steven Jobs
      c) Donald Trump
      d) William Gates

65.

When Soviet General Secretary Mikhail Gorbachev was to visit New York City, what did The Donald want him most to see?

a) The Statue of Liberty
b) MOMA
c) The New York Stock Exchange
d) Trump Tower
e) The whole concept of Trump Tower

Answer #64: a), b), and d). According to magazine TrumpProfiler John Taylor, Donald is not dreamy, but *is* soft and doughy. (If I were that little Pillsbury fellow I'd be careful!) [correct, 10 points; 8 penalty points if you blew it!!] _____ points earned. _____ running total.

Answer #65: You faithful TrumpWatchers have it right. It's e). [correct, 10 points; 7 penalty points if you blew this one!!] _____ points earned. _____ running total.

A TrumpFollow-Up

Question: Where does The Donald keep "the whole concept of Trump Tower"?
Answer: We don't know. But maybe it's with the Trump "concept of divorce" (Question #45) and the Trump "concept of cheating" (see below).

Trump on Fidelity!

"I don't like the *concept* of cheating."
[editors' note: emphasis added]

66.

A TrumpTriad!!

A. Question: How many times is Jack Nusbum mentioned in *Trump: The Art of the Deal*? (do not look at C. below!!!)

Answer (circle one):   105   54   9   0

B.   Question: Who is Jack Nusbaum?

Answer (about 2 sentences should do; if you have no idea at all who this Jack guy is, make up something and we'll see later about getting you a couple of points): _____

_____

_____ .

C. (You looked!!) Which of the answers below seems the best fit for the following question: "Why didn't The Donald tell us about Mr. Nusbaum in his book?"

a) Mr. Nusbaum is shy and The Donald wanted to protect his privacy.

b) Our source was wrong in this matter. (see answer to B for source)

c) Do you credit the cleaning lady in *Architectural Digest*?

d) Well, it's a semantic matter; I mean, what do you mean by help, what do you mean by deal, I mean, what do you mean by asking this kind of rude question anyhow?

e) Nusbaum is a man and an employee. You don't credit men, because they're the competition. Women, on the other hand, since they are not to be taken too seriously, can be praised to high heaven and no one will ever see them as a fantastic guy.

_____ points earned.   _____ running total.

Answer #66: A-0   B-sample two sentences follow: "The fifty-year-old lawyer, partner in Willkie Farr & Gallagher, is the brain behind the art of making the TrumpDeal, according to *Forbes*. The Donald tells Mr. Nusbaum what he wants to deal on and the lawyer tells The Donald how to do it."   C-Your guess is as good as ours! [10 points for getting A right, 50 points for whatever you entered for B and, if you actually got it right, take another 20 points, and on C simply take 5 points for our indecision; no penalty points on this one, no matter what you might have done!]

A TrumpLightningBolt

"Life is what you do while you're waiting to die."

67.

A TrumpSevenPointer!! Get all three of these TrumpQuestions correct and earn 7 points (that's right, 7)!

1.
What was the Steven Spielberg-Amy Irving divorce according to The Donald? (choose one)
a) "A damn shame."
b) "A film industry disaster."
c) "A one-day wonder."

2.
What was the Tom Hayden-Jane Fonda divorce according to The Donald? (choose one)
a) "The first sensible thing that woman's done in years."
b) "Typical California political-cinematic BS."
c) "A couple of inches in the *Daily News*."

3.
What was the Ivana-Donald separation and impending divorce according to The Donald?
a) "A story that won't quit."
b) "A monster in London."
c) "A nonevent."

Answer #67: 1-c   2-c   3-a, b, and c   [7 points if you got all three; 0 points if you missed any at all!!] _____ points earned. _____ running total.

XCVII

TDT's What's-Good-About-the-Japanese Quote

"Fortunately, they have a lot of money to spend, and they seem to like real estate."

TDT's What's-Bad-About-the-Japanese Quote

". . . they rarely smile and they are so serious that they don't make doing business fun."

TDT and Japanese Plant Life

"Trump went wild because he felt the tree was wrong, a hunchback, he wanted it pulled out. He wanted something like a sequoia."—New York City Parks Commissioner Henry Stern on the city's efforts to honor Trump by planting a delicate Japanese pine in his name

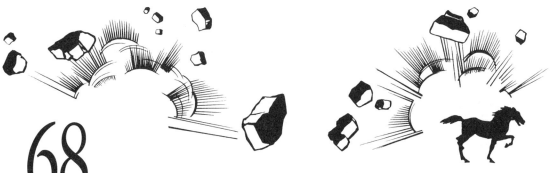

68.

What were the final words of Donald Trump about the Art Deco details on the old Bonwit Teller building in Manhattan when it was being torn down to make way for the classy, nothing-but-the-best Trump Tower?

a) "My goodness, we can't despoil art!! Let's give it to the Museum of Modern Art. They'll be so pleased."

b) "Can we get a deduction that will offset the cost of preserving this junk?"

c) "These decorations here, the classy ones, would make great earrings for my horsey wife."

d) "F— it; blow them up!"

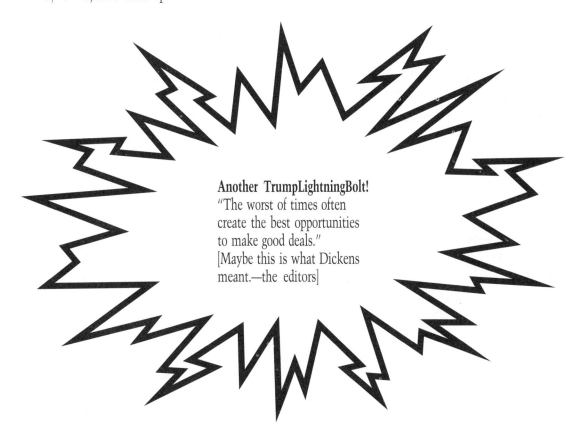

Another TrumpLightningBolt!
"The worst of times often create the best opportunities to make good deals."
[Maybe this is what Dickens meant.—the editors]

---

easy through here.] ____ points earned. ____ running total.

Answer #68: d) "F— it, blow them up!" [20 points for getting this one right, no penalty points, we need to take it

TrumpFacts!!!

#1. Because he's an obvious Trump insider (he's reportedly the brother of a supposedly former lover of Ivana's!), Mr. Ladislav Staidl is hard at work on a TV film about Ivana.

#2. In March 1990, a law firm hires a celebrity-look-alike agent to scour the country in search of Donald and Ivana Trump duplicates. When found, they're to be used to advertise the firm's divorce services.

#3. Funk and Wagnall defines *art* as "an aesthetically pleasing and meaningful arrangement of elements, as words, sounds, colors, shapes, etc." and *deal* as "to apportion to one his share." Thus, The Donald's autobiography, *The Art of the Deal*, could have simply been *The Aesthetically Pleasing and Meaningful Arrangement of Apportioning One His Share.*

A
YOU-KNOW-WHAT-WE-WISH?
Mini-Feature!!

We wish there was a Donald Trump Book
Feature in the newspapers, or maybe in
magazines, or maybe even on Television. It
would be a list of what books Mr. Donald
Trump is reading. That would be really
terrific, don't you think? Then we
TrumpAdmirers could all go out and read
the books that Donald Trump reads, and
maybe, just maybe, we would become just a
little bit more like him.   I mean, those
thoughts have to come from somewhere,
don't they?

69.

TrumpQuotes!! Of the following, only *one* is *not* a TrumpQuote! Find it!!

A. "I love to have enemies. I fight my enemies. I like beating my enemies to the ground."
B. "'Modest' isn't my favorite word."
C. "I feel sorry for Helmsley." [on Leona's Harry]
D. "Sorry I haven't called you back sooner, but I've been buying airlines . . . not bad for a kid from Queens, huh?"
E. "I like my oysters fried. That way I know they've died."
F. "There is no one my age who has accomplished more. . . . Everyone can't be the best."

70.

More TrumpQuotes! Which *one* of the following is *not* a TrumpQuote?!?

A. "They've got an arrogant head of the country, who I think is a total fool, and he's trying to make up for his losses by selling this technology [nuclear] to anyone, and it's a disgrace. It's a disgrace." [on France]
B. "Women. There's nothing they can do about it. The clock ticks and there's nothing they can do about it."
C. "Was it big over there in London, too? I heard it's a monster over there . . . it's unfortunate, I'd like it to go away. I'd like it to be a personal thing, privately done . . . one of the [New York] papers has twelve reporters on it!" [on his failed marriage]
D. "I guarantee they're going to sell the hell out of the newspaper today, in fact, I just got a call; you can't buy the *Post* anywhere. You can't buy it anywhere." [on the *New York Post's* "BEST SEX" headline]

Answer #69: E. "I like my oysters fried. That way I know they've died." [10 points for getting it right, and give yourself another 10 points if you thought that maybe this entry had something to do with Roy Blount!] points earned. _____ running total.

Answer #70: F. "Newspapermen ask dumb questions. They look up at the sun and ask you if the sun is shining." [This is a 40-pointer! 0 penalty points for blowing it, but give yourself another 5 bonus points if you thought this "newspapermen" entry had something to do with Sonny Liston.] _____ points earned. _____ running total.

E. "What they think doesn't matter. They have no power." [on a community group opposed to his building the world's tallest building in its neighborhood]

F. "Newspapermen ask dumb questions. They look up at the sun and ask you if the sun is shining." [on the media's response to the Trump breakup]

G. "It's really pretty sad, but it's been great for business." [on the blitz of publicity surrounding the failure of his marriage]

71.

Which of the following "is" or "is not" [i.e., simply "made up" for purpose of this really classy book] a selection from The Donald's introduction to "Trump: The Game"!!

	Is	Is Not
A. "I invite you to live the fantasy! Feel the power! And make the deals."	——	——
B. "Here's where shrewdness really pays off! . . . millions of dollars can be won or lost in seconds."	——	——
C. ". . . it's not whether you win or lose, but whether you win!"	——	——
D. "Victory goes to the player who makes the next-to-last mistake."	——	——
E. "This game is actually an outstanding innovation, derived from several closely related board games that have been popular in the Orient for centuries."	——	——

Answer #71: A-Is B-Is C-Is D-Is Not E-Is Not [10 points for each correct entry; 5 penalty points for each wrong answer!] ____ points earned. ____ running total.

CIII

TrumpInstruction!

72. If the Trump Taj Mahal is referred to as "The Eighth Wonder of the World" it is because:

a. The Sixth and Seventh have been disallowed.
b. It can somehow make over $1 million a day while surrounded by a medical-waste-infested ocean and a city rampant with crime, racial tension, poverty, and high unemployment.
c. Donald Trump's doing the referring.

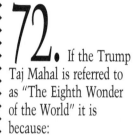
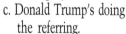

Answer #72: c. Donald Trump's doing the referring. [correct, 10 points; wrong, 0 points.] _____ points earned. _____ running total.

A TrumpQuote

". . . I could take it as a great compliment."

—**The Donald,** on the *New York Post's* front-page "BEST SEX" headline

73.

The Donald sued Eddie and Julius Trump for using their own name in their business—"The Trump Group"—and even though they'd been using that name for _____ years.

  a. 1
  b. 10
  c. 20
  d. 30
  e. 50

❀

Hi! My Name is_____

_____

Question: What did Adnan Khashoggi's apartment in Olympic Tower *used* to have?

Answer: The biggest living room that Donald Trump ever saw! But then . . .

running total.

Answer #73: c. 20 [correct, 20 points; wrong, -20 points!] _____ points earned.

CV

A TrumpDiscovery

Marble is a luxurious material, as we all know. It is hard to cut, hard to match, hard to finish, hard to clean, but the result is luxurious. Breccia Perniche is a rare marble that is a blend of rose, pink, and peach. Most of us would say pink. Let's say pink: It's a pink marble. Not only is it pink, it "literally takes your breath away," according to TDT. It has been our experience, however, that the literal breathtaking is barely noticeable because we have survived Trump Tower, that ravishing mall on Manhattan's fantastic Fifth Avenue where the walls and floors for six full floors are pink marble. But besides beauty and pinkness, there is another and nearly occult attribute of this fantastic material: It pumps people up to spend money! Now, guess who made that discovery? Right! Mr. Donald Trump.

74.

The Trumps Go Hollywood! Which one of the following is not actually part of the Trump influence on Hollywood?!?

a) The Donald played the part of "Mr. Spectacular" in the film *Ghosts Can't Do It.*

b) The Donald was featured in *I'll Take Manhattan,* the TV mini-series based on Judith Krantz's novel of the same title.

c) Ivana co-starred with Richard Simmons (and his mother) in the 1986 video hit "Downhill Ski to Fun and Slimness the Richard Simmons Way!"

d) The *Trump Princess* was featured in the James Bond film *Never Say Never.*

✂ COSMETIC SURGERY UPDATE ✂

"He definitely has not had anything done. I don't know when he would have had it; he's always working. He's never missed a day here."

—spokesperson for The Donald

"She's not had plastic surgery! She's lost a good ten pounds, switched to clothes by younger designers, and she's lightened up on her makeup."

—spokesperson for The Ivana

[10 points if you aced this one!] ——— points earned. ——— running total.

Answer #74: c) Ivana co-starred with Richard Simmons (and his mother) in the 1986 video hit "Downhill Ski to Fun and Slimness the Richard Simmons Way!"

A TrumpQuestion

Question: Who was The Donald's architect for the tasteful building that made him the figure he is today, and what is the half-kidding remark that all of us should remember?

Answer: Der Scutt. Honest. In response to a member of the community who was concerned that the building would steal even more sunlight from the area, Der Scutt (honest) said, "If you want sunlight, move to Kansas." (Who said wit was dead?)

A TrumpQuote!!

"I wouldn't bet

against her."

—The Donald, on

Ivana

75.

The Trumps Go Political! Which one of the following is not actually a Political TrumpQuote?!?

a) "I'm not running for president, but if I did, I'd win."—The Donald

b) "He'd love to be president, but only if he were appointed."—anonymous friend, on The Donald

c) "But there's no waterfall in that Oval Room?! And the neighborhood, that is not a good one!?"—Ivana, on potential conflicts should The Donald be president

d) "Can the First Lady run a casino?"—Ivana, on a potential conflict should The Donald be president

Answer #75: c) "But there's no waterfall in that Oval Room?! And the neighbor- hood, that is not a good one!?"—Ivana, on potential conflicts should The Donald be president [20 points for this one, no penalty for blowing it!] _____ points earned. _____ running total.

76.

Cross off the odd-one-out in the following TrumpGroupings!! [The first one is done for you!]

a) Johnny Carson ✦ Phyllis George ✦ ~~Michael Dukakis~~ ✦ David Merrick ✦ Paul Anka

b) Burger King ✦ Trumpet's ✦ Denny's ✦ McDonald's ✦ Wendy's ✦ White Tower

c) mirrors ✦ pink marble ✦ waterfalls ✦ Sears "Best Buy" wall paint

d) Tower Casino ✦ Taj Mahal ✦ Plaza ✦ Caramel Popcorn ✦ Parc ✦ City

e) Winkelmayr ✦ Trump ✦ Zelnicek ✦ Maples ✦ Zelnickova

f) Dodge Dart ✦ *Trump Princess* ✦ Yugo ✦ Plymouth Valiant ✦ Corvair

g) New York Military Academy ✦ Fordham ✦ Wharton ✦ PS 109

h) Trump ✦ Classy ✦ Chump ✦ Hump ✦ Dump ✦ Clump

TrumpGrammar

**"Whenever Walter Hoving saw a peddler, he'd go
to his people, and he'd start screaming, in his dignified
manner, 'How dare you let them do that?'"**

(As you likely know, there has been a good deal of debate about the use of the comma in the work of The Donald. The above sentence is a good example of what has spurred the debate. Some have suggested that Mr. Donald Trump does not know his commas. We are not of that school. The most reasonable construction is that he got a very good deal on a lot of commas at one time. There has also been some discussion of the use of irony in The Donald's oeuvre. We think it speaks for itself.)

running total _____

Answer #76: a) Michael Dukakis: he doesn't now nor has he ever owned a Trump Tower apartment. b) Trumpet's: it's a very *classy* restaurant with lots of *flair.* c) Sears "Best Buy" wall paint: it's not featured in TrumpProperties. d) Caramel Popcorn: it's not really a Trump. e) Maples: it's never been one of Ivana's last names according to *any* source. f) *Trump Princess:* it's a great boat, not a great car. g) PS 109: it's not part of The Donald's academic record. h) Classy: it doesn't rhyme with the others. [10 points for each correct answer; 0 points for each wrong answer, 50 bonus points if you got all these correct—wow!] _____ points earned.

CIX

A Trump Clarification

"My image is much different than I actually am."

—The Donald

A Swell
TrumpLightningBolt!

"There are always buyers for the best."

77. When a Chicago architecture critic characterized a Trump project as "architecturally lousy," what did DT do? (choose only one)
  a) suggested that the man be fired from his job at the *Chicago Tribune*
  b) sued him for $500 million
  c) wrote the offending Mr. Gapp a nice note suggesting that the building might shock at first but deserved a second look

Answer #77: b) If you thought the answer was a), you don't know our Donald! It is well known that Mr. Donald Trump reserves requests for firing for misinformed stock analysts who think it's a tad cool at New Jersey shore resorts in winter, for goodness' sake. [correct, 10 points, wrong, 0 points.] _____ points earned. _____ running total.

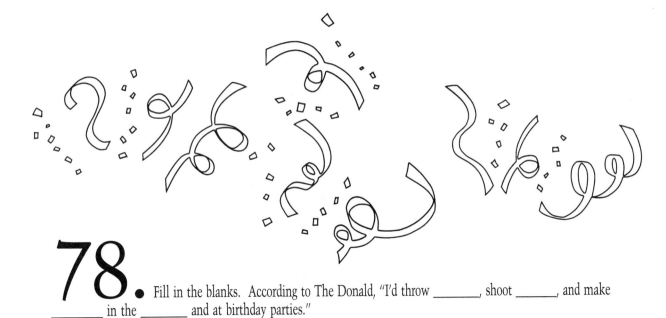

78.

Fill in the blanks. According to The Donald, "I'd throw _____, shoot _____, and make _____ in the _____ and at birthday parties."

a) cats, the moon, a fool of myself, media
b) fits, pigeons, a mess, boys' room
c) water balloons, spitballs, a ruckus, schoolyard
d) dwarfs, clay pigeons, big bucks, Caribbean

79.

Read the following specifications:

must be the largest,
gold-plated interior,
leather seating,
gourmet kitchen, and
an estimated construction cost of $20 million

and then choose the correct project which they describe:

a) the *Trump Princess*.
b) the *Trump Princess* replacement (no, this is not a pet name for an ex-industrial show mannequin)
c) a new place for Ivana
d) the proposed TrumpBlimp

Answer #78: c) water balloons, spitballs, a ruckus, schoolyard [correct, 10 points, wrong, 0 points.] _____ points earned. _____ running total.

Answer #79: d) is your answer. We did not include the fact that it would be filled with hot air, for that could be seen as a wise-guy *Fortune*-like disparagement of The Donald. [correct, 10 points, wrong, 0 points.] _____ points earned. _____ running total.

CXI

TRUMPLIGHTNINGBOLT

#1. "With such a great
location, the more apartments I
could build, the better the return
. . . on my investment."

#2. "Moreover, the higher I
could go, the better the
views—and the more I could
charge for the apartments."

80.

What or who was once called an "architectural bastard"?

a) Der Scutt
b) The Trump Taj Mahal
c) Paul Goldberger
d) Trump Tower
e) _____ [reader's choice]
f) Mar-a-Lago [Mr. Donald Trump's "greatest of the great houses" in exclusive Palm Beach]

TrumpFact!

On March 8, 1990, CBS News reports a Gallup poll that indicates that 55 percent of America's heads-of-households "have had enough" of the Trump separation/divorce story, while 10 percent "want even more." It was also noted that 37 percent of America's heads-of-households now know who Marla Maples is.

TrumpFiction!!

Ivana's former housekeeper from Montreal is hired (at the rate of $1,000 a day!!!) by a Chicago-based industrial toilet bowl cleanser firm to host their exhibit at various trade shows and show how "the rich, famous, and beautiful like to have theirs cleaned!"

Answer #80: *House and Garden* tells us that f) is correct. But then we can't rule out other possibilities. [Take 5 points no matter what you answered.] 5 points earned. _____ running total.

81.

What was Ivana referring to in the following sentence?

"We are secure people, so we didn't feel the need or the urge to put our personal stamp on it, because it was already very beautiful."

a) The *Trump Princess*
b) The Plaza
c) Notre-Dame de Paris
d) New York City
e) Mar-a-Lago

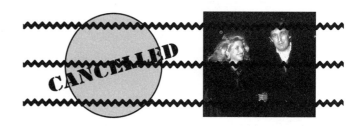

82.

Had Donald Trump done any extraterrestrial traveling?

a) yes
b) no
c) we can't say for sure

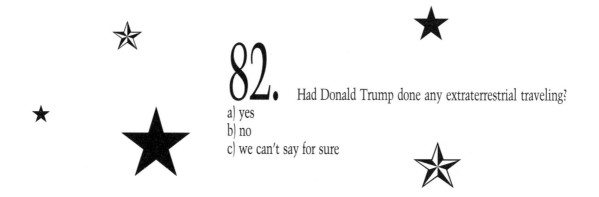

Answer #81: The *Princess* and the Plaza (ooh, what a good name for a television series) and New York City have all had the benefit of the Trump personal stamp. As of this writing neither of the independent Trumps has even made an offer on Notre-Dame de Paris in Paris, France. So e) is the answer, Mar-a-Lago, the architectural bastard by the sea. [correct, 10 points; wrong, 0 points.] _____ points earned. _____ running total.

Answer #82: c) We can't say for sure, but the suspicion is that he has. Otherwise he would have been talking through his hat or dealing in vulgar hyperbole, two things we very much doubt, when he said in 1987 that Trump Tower is "the most sucessful building in the universe." (You just have to ferret out this stuff when a guy is so private, you know?) [correct, 10 points; wrong, 0 points] _____ points earned _____ running total.

TEST RESULTS

Enter your total points: _____

• If you scored between -133 and 1000 you ought to seek help. Serious help. Of some sort. Of any sort.

• Between 1000 and 3000 you are simply not paying attention. Where have you been for the last ten years?—the last ten months? Why did you even do this test? You obviously really don't care about the Trumps—and that is incredible!

• Between 3000 and 5000—now you're showing some class! A bit of flair! A touch of glitz!

• And if you scored 5000 or higher, you're obviously a TrumpExpert!! Congratulations!! [But you're spending too damn much time reading stuff like *People*, the *New York Daily News*, *Star*, the *National Enquirer*, and the *New York Post*. Might we suggest a Dickens novel, or your trying shorter checkout lines.]

TrumpFacts—A Couple of Them!!

#1.
On the *Trump Princess*, the house-keeping [yachtkeeping?] crew has to vacuum the carpeting backward, then back themselves out of each room, because Ivana likes to walk on carpeting when it's fresh.

#2.
On March 1, 1990, a Las Vegas bookie offers odds on the next Mrs. Trump:

Marla Maples	50-1
Priscilla Presley	100-1
Kim Basinger	100-1
Leona Helmsley	1 billion-1

TrumpFinals!!!

A Final Trump Definition

Question: What is the difference between glitz and flash?
Answer: Glitz, according to The Donald, is what he uses in his casinos. Flash is what he uses in some of his residential buildings. It is "a level below glitz."

A Final TrumpSurprise

The object of "Trump: The Game" is to (get a load of this!) "have the most money at the end of the game!"

A Final TrumpMini-Feature

Total Number of Rooms Inhabited by The Trumps:
47 (Connecticut home)
+ 118 (Florida home)
+ 100 (Manhattan home)

———————————————————

265 total rooms inhabited by Trumps!!

A Final TrumpNote

Ivana pronounces "Marla" as "Moola."

Whither
The
Donald?

With the unfortunate Ms. Maples affair and the attendant impending divorce proceedings, the *Playboy* cover with the clearly underdressed lady, and the opening of the Trump Taj, the enemies of Donald had a field day. In his forays into television where, much against his natural bent, The Donald submitted to interviews to set the record straight about the actual size of his, uh, fortune, the image of Mr. Donald Trump as a silly, rich, even pitiful bag of flatulent wind was fostered by the media. For us DonaldDevotees, however, the truth lay elsewhere. (Or something lay elsewhere. What was it? Oh, yes, Donald lay elsewhere.) The whole point of TD's being was lost on the superficial press. The fact was and is that Mr. Donald Trump had become the great ironist of our time. There could be no other explanation of his behavior.

Who else but a great ironist making of his life a piece of performance art would say the things he had said? How else to explain the denial of cold and dreary winter weather at the Jersey shore, the allegiance to the *concept* of fidelity while allegedly carrying on an affair with a former trade show mannequin? What else could possibly be the root of the need to convert goods into cash couched in terms of opportunity; why else pooh-pooh the *Forbes* discussion of the diminution of his wealth by half in under a year? Who else—please, God, tell me—who else would have his lawyer inform all of us that The Donald and his wife had signed a nonfidelity agreement good for 60 days!! (Is it renewable and is there a pick of the litter clause?) Only The Best, The Greatest, The Supreme Ironist, that's who! And who else is The Supreme Ironist, ladies and gentlemen, than our own Mr. Donald Trump?

After all of the time we have devoted to the careful observation and emulation of our Donald, we have joyfully concluded that his larger-than-tabloid life that has riveted the attention of America and the world for over a decade has all been a brilliant and carefully played ironic performance by a master.

And so we come to the end of the story. The end of the story?!! Of course not; not the literal end of the story, because—all together now—*this story won't quit!* No, we just reach the end of the book. (You know, a book can be great, fabulous, and incredible, but you have to be cost effective, you know what I mean? The book gets longer, costs more to print, the cover price goes up, and before you know it, you have consumer resistance, right? We wouldn't want that. This book, as you may have noted, does not have lots of windows with a great view of the greatest city in the world. After all, how many rich, red-sports-car-driving Italians with blonde wives are there?)

We come to the end knowing that The Donald will keep on giving the ironic lessons he has been giving. One is his new book, which he ironically calls "trenchant" (what a genius at the put-on!), coming from Random House the very season this book appears!!! (Can you stand the anticipation? My God, just thinking about the LightningBolts in our future makes us lose our breath just the way we lose our breath when in the company of pink marble.)

And so, Dear Readers, we leave fair TrumpLand with:

The Final TrumpQuote

"You know, it is all a rather sad situation."

PHOTO CREDITS